Frommer's

Zion & Bryce Canyon National Parks

8th Edition

by Don & Barbara Laine

WILEY

John Wiley & Sons, Inc.

ABOUT THE AUTHORS

Residents of northern New Mexico since 1970, **Don and Barbara Laine** have traveled extensively throughout the Rocky Mountains and the Southwest, spending as much time as possible in the outdoors, and especially in the region's national parks and monuments. They have written Frommer's guides to Utah, Colorado, and the National Parks of the American West. The Laines have also authored *Little-Known Southwest, New Mexico & Arizona State Parks,* and *Best Short Hikes in Arizona* for The Mountaineers, and *The New Mexico Guide* for Fulcrum Publishing.

Published by:
JOHN WILEY & SONS, INC.
111 River St.
Hoboken, NJ 07030-5774

ISBN 978-1-118-11803-0 (paper); 978-1-118-22447-2 (ebk); 978-1-118-23777-9 (ebk); 978-1-118-26264-1 (ebk)

Editor: Alexia Travaglini
Production Editor: M. Faunette Johnston
Cartographer: Andy Dolan
Photo Editor: Richard Fox
Production by Wiley Indianapolis Composition Services

Front cover photo: Court of the Patriarchs mountains, Zion National Park
© Blickwinkel / Alamy Images.

For information on our other products and services or to obtain technical support, please contact our Customer Care Department within the U.S. at 877/762-2974, outside the U.S. at 317/572-3993 or fax 317/572-4002.

Wiley also publishes its books in a variety of electronic formats. Some content that appears in print may not be available in electronic formats.

Manufactured in the United States of America

5   4   3   2   1

CONTENTS

LIST OF MAPS

TRAVEL RESOURCES AT FROMMERS.COM

Frommer's travel resources don't end with this guide. Frommer's web-site, **www.frommers.com**, has travel information on more than 4,000 destinations. We update features regularly, giving you access to the most current trip-planning information and the best airfare, lodging, and car-rental bargains. You can also listen to podcasts, connect with other Frommers.com members through our active-reader forums, share your travel photos, read blogs from guidebook editors and fellow travelers, and much more.

HOW TO CONTACT US

In researching this book, we discovered many wonderful places—hotels, restaurants, shops, and more. We're sure you'll find others. Please tell us about them, so we can share the information with your fellow travelers in upcoming editions. If you were disappointed with a recommendation, we'd love to know that, too. Please write to:

Frommer's Zion & Bryce Canyon National Parks, 8th Edition
John Wiley & Sons, Inc. • 111 River St. • Hoboken, NJ 07030-5774
frommersfeedback@wiley.com

AN ADDITIONAL NOTE

Travel information can change quickly and unexpectedly, and we strongly advise you to confirm important details locally before traveling, including information on visas, health and safety, traffic and transport, accommodations, shopping, and eating out. We also encourage you to stay alert while traveling and to remain aware of your surroundings. Avoid civil disturbances, and keep a close eye on cameras, purses, wallets, and other valuables.

FROMMER'S STAR RATINGS, ICONS & ABBREVIATIONS

Every hotel, restaurant, and attraction listing in this guide has been ranked for quality, value, service, amenities, and special features using a **star-rating system.** In country, state, and regional guides, we also rate towns and regions to help you narrow down your choices and budget your time accordingly. Hotels and restaurants are rated on a scale of zero (recommended) to three stars (exceptional). Attractions, shopping, nightlife, towns, and regions are rated according to the following scale: zero stars (recommended), one star (highly recommended), two stars (very highly recommended), and three stars (must-see).

In addition to the star-rating system, we also use **seven feature icons** that point you to the great deals, in-the-know advice, and unique experiences that separate travelers from tourists. Throughout the book, look for:

special finds—those places only insiders know about

fun facts—details that make travelers more informed and their trips more fun

kids—best bets for kids and advice for the whole family

special moments—those experiences that memories are made of

overrated—places or experiences not worth your time or money

insider tips—great ways to save time and money

 great values—where to get the best deals

The following abbreviations are used for credit cards:

AE American Express	DISC Discover	V Visa
DC Diners Club	MC MasterCard	

INTRODUCING ZION & BRYCE CANYON NATIONAL PARKS

There aren't many places in the world where the forces of nature have come together with such dramatic results as in Zion and Bryce Canyon national parks. From arid desert to pine-covered peaks and awe-inspiring rock formations, these parks offer some of the American West's most spectacular scenery, plus almost unlimited opportunities for hiking, camping, and other outdoor experiences.

Zion and Bryce Canyon sit on the vast Colorado Plateau, which they share with Utah's three other national parks (Arches, Canyonlands, and Capitol Reef) and Grand Canyon National Park, in Arizona.

The plateau began millions of years ago when forces deep within the earth forced the crust to rise, exposing many strata of rocks, and erosion and weathering sculpted rock formations, colored with an iron-rich palette of reds, oranges, pinks, and browns.

Both national parks are known for their stunning geology—Zion for massive sandstone monoliths and Bryce for delicate limestone sculptures called hoodoos. But there are also shimmering pools of deep green water, a roaring river, forests of pine and fir, and a vast array of plants and animals.

ACTIVE PURSUITS The main activities in both parks are enjoying the delightful and awe-inspiring scenery—from the convenience of designated viewpoints and the scenic drives—and hiking. There is plenty to see from the roads and short walks, and the more adventurous will savor challenging hiking trails and backcountry routes. You can also experience a bit of the Old West while seeing the parks' scenery by horseback— guided rides are offered at both parks.

Bryce Canyon is a bit more user-friendly than Zion, while Zion offers a greater variety of features to explore, from river canyons with colorful gardens to rocky windswept ridges. Bryce also has several fairly easy trails that lead right into the middle of some of its best scenery. This isn't to say that Zion is hard to get into, but because of the greater variety of terrain it takes a bit more time and effort to achieve that same feeling that you *know* the park.

FLORA & FAUNA   While best known for its massive rock formations, Zion National Park also has an abundance of wildlife. Watch for **mule deer** and **desert Bighorn sheep,** and also for the **chuckwalla,** a lizard that can grow to 20 inches long. Zion has over 900 species of plants. Watch for spring lines and their lush hanging gardens, clinging to the sides of cliffs. Summer visitors are bound to see the **sacred datura,** with large, funnel-shaped white flowers.

Bryce Canyon National Park's wildlife ranges from **mule deer**—which seem to be everywhere—to the **golden-mantled ground squirrel** and **Uinta chipmunk.** Watch for **white-throated swifts** as they perform exotic acrobatics along cliff faces. In the high mountains of Bryce Canyon is a forest of fir and spruce, with stands of quaking **aspen** that turn a magnificent bright yellow each fall. Along the exposed, rocky slopes here you will also find **bristlecone pine,** the oldest single organism known.

TOURS   In addition to the tours by horse offered at both parks by **Canyon Trail Rides,** there are excellent free ranger programs.

At Zion National Park, **ranger programs** include a 2-hour **Ride with a Ranger** shuttle-bus trip, which offers an opportunity to see Zion Canyon from a park ranger's unique perspective (reservations required). The **Zion Canyon Field Institute** offers outdoor workshops and classes, including **photo workshops** led by institute director Michael Plyler, a skilled professional photographer.

Ranger programs at Bryce Canyon National Park include various walks and hikes, such as a wheelchair-accessible, 1.5-hour **canyon rim walk** and a **moonlight hike.** Especially popular are the park's **Astronomy Programs,** usually offered 3 nights a week through the summer. Telescopes are provided. Sign up in advance at the visitor center.

INTRODUCING ZION & BRYCE CANYON NATIONAL PARKS | Introduction

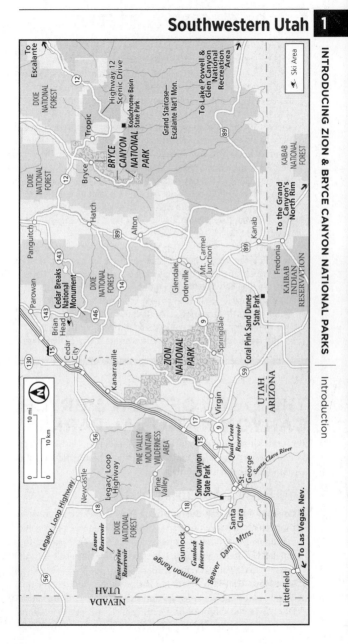

3

💬 butch cassidy SLEPT HERE

Robert LeRoy Parker wasn't a bad kid. He was born into a hard-working Mormon family, in the little Southwestern Utah town of Beaver, on April 13, 1866. The oldest of 13 children, Robert was said to be a great help to his mother, and worked on the small ranch his parents bought near Circleville, about 50 miles north of Bryce Canyon.

It was in Circleville where the problems began. Teenager Robert fell in with some rather unsavory characters, including one Mike Cassidy, the ne'er-do-well role model who reportedly gave the youth his first gun, and presumably from whom young Robert took the alias "Cassidy." The boy made his way to Telluride, Colorado, worked for one of the mines there for a while, and then wandered up to Wyoming. A little more wandering took him back to Telluride—and, strangely enough, the Telluride bank was robbed. Butch Cassidy had officially begun his life of crime.

In the following years, Butch—who gained the nickname after a short stint working in a butcher shop—became an expert at rustling cattle, robbing banks, and, his ultimate glory, robbing trains. Butch wanted to call his gang the Train Robbers Syndicate, but they raised such hell in celebration of their economic successes that saloonkeepers in Vernal and other Utah towns began calling them "that wild bunch," and the name stuck. The Wild Bunch would travel through Utah, hiding out in the desolate badlands that were

THE best OF ZION & BRYCE CANYON NATIONAL PARKS

Because planning a trip here can be bewildering, with so many options, we've assembled the very best that these parks and the surrounding areas have to offer.

The Best Day Hikes

o **Emerald Pools Trail System** (Zion National Park): If green is your color, you'll love this trail—algae keep the three pools glowing a deep, rich, and yes, emerald green. The first part of the trail leads through a forest to the Lower Emerald Pool, with its lovely waterfall and hanging garden. See p. 37.

o **East Mesa Trail** (Zion National Park): Allow a full day for this 6-mile hike, which is an easier and shorter route to Observation Point than the Observation Point Trail. From the promontory, you'll get spectacular views down Zion Canyon, with the Great to become Bryce Canyon, Capitol Reef, and Canyonlands national parks. Capitol Reef's Cassidy Arch was named after Butch; this area was supposedly one of his favorite hiding places.

If you've seen the 1969 movie *Butch Cassidy and the Sundance Kid,* with Paul Newman as Butch and Robert Redford as his partner-in-crime Sundance, you can't forget the spectacular scene in which Butch and his cohorts blow the door off a railroad car. Then they use way too much dynamite to open the safe, sending bills flying into the air. Apparently, the story is basically true, having taken place on June 2, 1899, near Wilcox, Wyoming. According to reports of the day, they got away with $30,000.

The Union Pacific Railroad took exception to Butch's antics. When the posse started getting a bit too close, Butch, Sundance, and Sundance's lady friend, Etta Place (Katharine Ross in the film), took off for South America, where it's said they continued a life of crime for a half dozen or so years.

According to some historians (as well as the movie), Butch and Sundance were shot dead in a gun battle with army troops in Bolivia in 1908. But others say it's not so; the other theory is that Butch returned to the United States, visited friends and family in Utah and Wyoming, and eventually settled in Spokane, Washington, where he lived a peaceful and respectable life under the name William T. Phillips, until he died of cancer in 1937.

White Throne in the foreground and Red Arch Mountain beyond. See p. 43.

o **Navajo Loop/Queen's Garden Trails** (Bryce Canyon National Park): To truly experience magical Bryce Canyon, you should hike down into it, and this not-too-difficult, 3-mile combination of trails is the perfect way to go. Start at Sunset Point and get the steepest part out of the way first. You'll see Thor's Hammer, the towering skyscrapers of Wall Street, and some of the park's most fanciful formations, including majestic Queen Victoria. See p. 83.

o **Rim Trail** (Bryce Canyon National Park): This underrated trail is a delight, providing splendid views down into spectacularly scenic Bryce Amphitheater from a variety of vantage points over its 5½-mile length. More walking than hiking, the Rim Trail includes a half-mile section between two overlooks—Sunrise and Sunset—that is suitable for wheelchairs. Views are especially fine early in the morning, when you can watch the changing light on the red rocks below. See p. 86.

The Best Backcountry Hikes

o **Hiking the Narrows** (Zion National Park): This is an experience unique to Zion National Park—a hike through a 1,000-foot-deep canyon, with water filling it from side to side in most places. Although much of Zion is dry rock, this is anything but, and it's an incredible experience for people in good shape and with strong nerves. It can be experienced in three ways—as a short day hike, a full-day hike, or an overnight hike—but all involve getting wet. *Warning:* The Narrows is prone to flash flooding, so check weather forecasts and flash-flood potential before setting out. See p. 48.

o **Riggs Spring Loop Trail** (Bryce Canyon National Park): Although this 9-mile loop can be hiked in 1 day, it's better as an overnight backpacking trip. This enables you to take your time to see wildlife (possibly even mountain lions), as you hike through forests of Douglas fir, ponderosa pines, piñon, and aspen, with views of the white and pink cliffs soaring above. See p. 87.

The Best Wildlife Viewing Spots

Check out chapter 9 for a complete guide to the flora and fauna of both parks.

o **Angels Landing Trail** (Zion National Park): The difficult hike on this trail provides opportunities to see mule deer, golden eagles, peregrine falcons, and lizards; it also offers splendid views into Zion Canyon. *Warning:* The last half-mile of this trail is along a knife-edge ridge—*definitely* not for anyone with even a mild fear of heights. See p. 35.

o **Riverside Walk** (Zion National Park): Here, near the entrance to the Narrows, deep in a slot canyon carved by the Virgin River, you're apt to see the American dipper bird—also called the water ouzel—as it dives into the water in search of aquatic insects. This is also the only place in the world where you'll find the Zion snail, although it may be hard to recognize—it's only ⅛th inch across. *Warning:* Because the Narrows is prone to flash flooding, check weather forecasts carefully before setting out. See p. 38.

o **Weeping Rock Area** (Zion National Park): Easily accessible via a short but steep paved trail, Weeping Rock oozes water that nurtures lush hanging gardens and produces the perfect habitat for a variety of wildlife, especially birds. Watch for peregrine falcons, American dippers, canyon wrens, and white-throated swifts. See p. 41.

- **Riggs Spring Loop Trail** (Bryce Canyon National Park): This little-used backcountry trail through woodland provides an opportunity to see a variety of wildlife, possibly even one of the park's elusive mountain lions. See p. 87.

- **Campgrounds** (both Zion and Bryce Canyon national parks): It couldn't be easier to see wildlife. Simply sit quietly at your campsite, preferably when few people are in the campground, and wait. You'll see Uinta chipmunks in both parks, white-tailed antelope squirrels at Zion, and golden-mantled ground squirrels at Bryce Canyon. There are almost always plenty of birds, and you're also apt to see mule deer, especially in Watchman Campground at Zion National Park. See chapters 4 and 7 for campground information.

The Best Scenic Views

- **Zion Canyon Scenic Drive** (Zion National Park): The 12-mile round-trip drive through Zion Canyon is impressive no matter how you do it—in your own vehicle (in winter only) or on the shuttle from spring through fall. In every direction the views are awe-inspiring, as the massive stone formations reach for the heavens. The road also provides easy access to a number of wonderful viewpoints and trail heads just off the roadway. See p. 23.

- **Angels Landing** (Zion National Park): The strenuous Angels Landing Trail leads across a high narrow ridge to a spectacular and dizzying view of Zion Canyon. *Warning:* The last half-mile of this trail is along a knife-edge ridge—*definitely* not for anyone with a fear of heights. See p. 35.

- **The Narrows** (Zion National Park): The sheer 1,000-foot-high walls are awe-inspiring, almost frightening, as they enclose you in a narrow world of hanging gardens, waterfalls, and sculpted sandstone arches, with the Virgin River pouring over and around your feet and legs—but the views make it worth getting wet. *Warning:* Because the Narrows is prone to flash flooding, check weather forecasts carefully before setting out. See p. 26 and p. 48.

- **Inspiration Point** (Bryce Canyon National Park): An appropriately named stop, Inspiration Point provides a phenomenal view down into Bryce Amphitheater, the park's largest and most colorful natural amphitheater. From here, you see the Silent City, packed with hoodoos (rock formations) that inspire the imagination. Some like the view even better just south of Inspiration Point, along the Rim Trail, up a little rise, at what is usually called Upper Inspiration Point. See p. 73.

o **Queen's Garden Trail** (Bryce Canyon National Park): Presided over by majestic Queen Victoria, the thousands of colorful and intricately sculpted spires present a magnificent display when viewed from the rim. From this trail below, they're even better. See p. 74 and p. 83.

o **The Rim at Sunrise** (Bryce Canyon National Park): If you thought the hoodoos were magnificent in the full light of day, wait until you see them glowing with the deep colors of the morning sun as it rises slowly above the rim. The changing angle of light creates a constantly moving panorama of shadow and color. Walk along the Rim Trail or stop at the viewpoints along the northern half of the park's scenic drive. See p. 86 for the Rim Trail; see chapter 6 for information on the scenic drive.

The Best Natural Spectacles

o **The Great White Throne** (Zion National Park): A huge white monolith, the Great White Throne demands attention as soon as you glimpse it. Considered the symbol of Zion National Park, this massive block of Navajo sandstone towers 2,000 feet high, and can be seen from the scenic drive as well as from several hiking trails, including Observation Point Trail, Deertrap Mountain Trail, Angels Landing Trail, and Emerald Pools Trail. See chapters 3 and 4 for descriptions of the Great White Throne and the trails that give you the best vantage points.

o **The Narrows** (Zion National Park): It's difficult to comprehend that this beautiful canyon, 1,000 feet deep and less than 20 feet wide in places, was carved from solid stone, beginning millions of years ago, by the often gently flowing Virgin River at your feet. But to see the flip side of the river, just wait for a rainstorm; it becomes an angry, destructive force that you can well imagine would slice through anything that got in its way. *Warning:* Because the Narrows is prone to flash flooding, check weather forecasts carefully before setting out. See p. 26 and p. 48.

o **Queen Victoria** (Bryce Canyon National Park): Among the most impressive hoodoos in the park, from the correct angle, this honestly looks just like the photos of England's Queen Victoria that you see in books and magazines. It even has the same air of superiority. See p. 83.

o **Bryce Amphitheater Capped with Snow** (Bryce Canyon National Park): The hoodoos become transformed into intricately carved creatures topped with white icing, a fairyland in orange and white. You'll get great views from stops along the scenic drive and by walking the Rim Trail. See p. 86 for the Rim Trail; see chapter 6 for information on the scenic drive.

The Best Winter Sports Location

o **Fairyland Loop Trail** (Bryce Canyon National Park): There aren't many cross-country ski trails that can match Bryce Canyon's Fairyland Loop for scenic beauty. The trail leads 1 mile through a pine and juniper forest to the Fairyland Point Overlook, with spectacular views into Bryce Amphitheater, where a blanket of snow adorns the multicolored hoodoos with a sparkling white mantle. See p. 85.

The Best Children's & Family Experiences

o **Junior Rangers/Explorers Program** (Zion National Park): Although Junior Rangers programs are available at most national parks, the one offered at Zion each summer is quite extensive, with both morning and afternoon activities that teach kids what makes this natural wonder so special. See p. 33.

o **Weeping Rock Trail** (Zion National Park): This short hike on a paved trail has interpretive signs explaining the natural history of the area. But the best part is at the end, when the trail arrives at a rock alcove with lush hanging gardens of ferns and wildflowers, where you can lift your face to receive a cooling spray of mist from above. See p. 41.

o **Queen's Garden Trail** (Bryce Canyon National Park): Not only is this trail fairly easy, but it drops down into one of the most scenic parts of the park, meandering among unique and oddly carved hoodoos. It's fun to let your imagination run wild, both for youngsters and the kid in all of us. See p. 83.

The Best Drive-In Camping

o **Watchman Campground** (Zion National Park): Located just inside the park's south entrance, Watchman Campground has well-spaced sites and lots of trees. In addition, this campground is near the park shuttle terminal, providing easy access to the popular upper Zion Canyon section of the park. And it even has electric hookups for RVs, a rarity in national parks. See p. 62.

o **North Campground** (Bryce Canyon National Park): While both of Bryce Canyon National Park's campgrounds offer plenty of trees, providing that genuine "forest camping" experience, North Campground is closer to the Rim Trail than the park's other campground, making it easier to rush over to catch those amazing sunrise colors. See p. 97.

o **Ruby's Inn RV Park & Campground** (near Bryce Canyon National Park): For those who want full RV hookups, a woodsy camping experience, lots of amenities, and easy access to the national park, this is the place to be. Part of a giant complex containing a motel, shops, swimming pools, and all sorts of other attractions and activities, this campground has trees and open space as well. See p. 97.

The Best Backcountry Camping

o **La Verkin Creek/Kolob Arch Trails** (Zion National Park): You'll have to sign up in advance for one of the isolated campsites along this spectacularly scenic trail in the Kolob Canyons. The trail takes you through forests of conifers, cottonwoods, and box elders, past hanging gardens and a series of waterfalls. There is also a side trip to a view of Kolob Arch—at over 300 feet wide, one of the largest natural arches in the world. See p. 48.

The Best Lodging

o **Zion Lodge** (Zion National Park; ☏ **435/772-7700**): The handsome Zion Lodge was built by the Union Pacific Railroad in 1925. Tragedy struck in 1966, when it was destroyed by fire. However, it was rebuilt the following year in its original style, and continues to offer the best lodging and location in Zion. Situated in a forest with spectacular views of the park's rock cliffs, it offers both cabins and motel rooms. Each of the charming cabins has a private porch, stone (gas-burning) fireplace, two double beds, and log beams. See p. 55.

o **Flanigan's Inn** (near Zion National Park; ☏ **800/765-7787** or 435/772-3244): Made of natural wood and rock, and set among trees, lawns, and flowers just outside the entrance to Zion National Park, this very attractive complex has a mountain-lodge atmosphere. It's a place where you actually want to spend some time—unlike some other area options, which are just good places to crash at the end of a busy day. See p. 58.

o **The Lodge at Bryce Canyon** (Bryce Canyon National Park; ☏ **435/834-8700**): This handsome sandstone and ponderosa pine lodge is the perfect place to stay while visiting the park. Opened in 1924, it has all the atmosphere of the 1920s, but it also has most of the modern conveniences people expect today. Especially recommended are its delightful cabins, which have been authentically restored and contain gas-burning stone fireplaces. Those wanting a bit more elegance will enjoy one of the lodge's suites, which are decorated with white wicker furnishings and have ceiling fans and separate sitting areas. See p. 93.

o **Best Western Plus Ruby's Inn** (near Bryce Canyon National Park; ☏ **866/866-6616** or 435/834-5341): The motel rooms here are fine—clean and well maintained, with color TVs, telephones, and air-conditioning—but the real reason to stay here is the location, just outside the park entrance. Numerous amenities are offered, from swimming pools and restaurants to shuttle service. This place has an incredible tour desk to book activities. See p. 94.

o **Stone Canyon Inn** (near Bryce Canyon National Park; ✆ 866/489-4680): Quiet seclusion, loads of charm, and absolutely splendid views are only three of the reasons we highly recommend this inn—it is also very upscale and *the* place to come to be pampered. Each of the six guest rooms is unique, with queen- or king-size beds, handsome wood furnishings, and a classic Western look. The luxurious cottages each have two bedrooms and two bathrooms, a gas fireplace, full kitchen, and a private deck with a hot tub. See p. 96.

The Best Restaurants

o **Bit & Spur Restaurant & Saloon** (near Zion National Park; ✆ 435/772-3498): Although this looks like a rough-and-tumble Old West saloon at first glance, it's really a very good restaurant, similar to one of the better restaurants in Santa Fe. The menu includes Mexican standards such as burritos, flautas, and traditional chili stew, but you'll also find more exotic creations. Portions are generous. See p. 64.

o **The Lodge at Bryce Canyon** (Bryce Canyon National Park; ✆ 435/834-8700): A delightful mountain-lodge atmosphere and very good food make this restaurant a winner. Decorated with American Indian weavings and baskets, the restaurant has two large stone fireplaces and picture windows looking out at the park. The menu changes periodically but usually has items such as Alaskan sockeye salmon topped with sun-dried-tomato pesto, rack of lamb, and steaks, including a bison tenderloin. There are also pasta and vegetarian dishes. Then there are the lodge's specialty ice creams and desserts, such as the exotic and very tasty wild "Bryceberry" bread pudding. See p. 100.

o **Red Rock Grill in Zion Lodge** (Zion National Park; ✆ 435/772-3213): You can't beat the view here—large picture windows face the park's magnificent rock formations—and the food is pretty special, too. Try the Santa Fe flatiron steak or the very popular trout amandine. See p. 64.

The Best Side Trips

o **Cedar Breaks National Monument** (near Cedar City, a side trip from Zion National Park): A delightful little park, Cedar Breaks

National Monument is a junior Bryce Canyon, with a spectacular natural amphitheater filled with stone spires, arches, and columns, and painted in reds, purples, oranges, and ochers. You can camp among the spruce, firs, and wildflowers that blanket the 10,000-foot plateau each summer. See p. 108.

o **Grand Staircase–Escalante National Monument** (near Bryce Canyon National Park): This vast wilderness, covering almost 1.9 million acres, is known for its stark, rugged beauty, including striking red-orange canyons and deep river valleys. Unlike most other national monuments, almost all of this sweeping area is undeveloped—there are few all-weather roads, only one maintained hiking trail, and two small developed campgrounds. But for the adventurous, there are miles upon miles of dirt roads and practically unlimited opportunities for hiking, horseback riding, camping, and exploring. See p. 112.

A LOOK AT ZION

While it may be easy to conjure up a single defining image of the enormous Grand Canyon or the delicately sculpted rock hoodoos of Bryce, Zion is more difficult to pin down. Here you'll find a collage of images and secrets, an entire smorgasbord of experiences, sights, and even smells, from massive stone sculptures and monuments to lush forests and roaring rivers. Zion is a park to explore, not merely to see; take time to walk its trails, visit viewpoints at different times of the day to see the changing light, and let the park work its magic on you.

First established as Mukuntuweep National Monument in 1909—*mukuntuweep* is a Paiute Indian word meaning "straight arrow"—its name was changed to Zion National Monument in 1918, and the area gained national park status the following year. Comprising more than 147,000 acres, the park covers a wide range of elevations—from 3,700 to 8,726 feet above sea level—and terrain that runs the gamut from desert to forest, with a dramatic river canyon known as the Narrows thrown in for good measure.

These extremes of elevation have resulted in extremes of climate as well—temperatures in the desert areas soar to well over 100°F (38°C) in the summer, while higher elevations are sometimes covered with snow and ice in the winter. Due to this variety of conditions, Zion harbors a vast array of plant life, ranging from cactus and yucca to ponderosa pines and cottonwoods. In fact, with almost 800 native species, Zion National Park is said to have the richest diversity of plants in Utah. Be sure to watch for hanging gardens, kept alive with water from porous rocks, which you'll see clinging to the sides of cliffs.

Impressions

Nothing can exceed the wondrous beauty of Zion . . . in the nobility and beauty of the sculptures, there is no comparison.
—Geologist Clarence Dutton, 1880

Zion is also home to a great variety of animals, drawn here in large part by the year-round water source. Indigenous mammals range from pocket gophers to mountain lions; you'll also spy hundreds of birds, lizards of all shapes and sizes, and a dozen species of snakes. (Only the Great Basin rattlesnake is poisonous, and it usually slithers away from you faster than you can run from it.) Mule deer are commonly observed grazing along the forest edges, and practically every park visitor comes across squirrels and chipmunks. A few elk and bighorn sheep may surface, although they're seldom seen. Among the creatures unique to the park is the tiny Zion snail. See chapter 10 for more details on the flora and fauna of the parks.

Of course, it's not only plants and animals that need water. For some 1,500 years, humans have come here seeking not only water but also the plants and animals that the water nurtures. There is evidence that a group of people, known as the Basket Makers, lived here as early as A.D. 500, hunting the area's wildlife, gathering berries and seeds, and growing corn, squash, and other crops. They apparently abandoned the area about A.D. 1200, perhaps because of climate changes. Members of the American Indian Paiute tribe—whose descendants still live in southern Utah—are believed to have spent time in what is now the national park, but built no permanent homes. Spanish explorers were in the area in the late 18th century, and American fur traders came in the early 19th century, but there is no evidence that either actually entered what is now Zion Canyon National Park proper.

Historians believe that it was not until the 1850s that European-Americans finally ventured into Zion Canyon. Probably the first was pioneer Nephi Johnson, who was shown Zion Canyon by Paiutes in November 1858, and for whom Johnson Mountain is named. He was among a group of members of the Church of Jesus Christ of Latter-day Saints (also known as Mormons) that was sent from Salt Lake City by church leader Brigham Young in search of arable land. By the early 1860s, the Mormons had begun to establish farms and ranches in the area, near where Zion Lodge is located today and at other locations in what is now the national park. It was early Mormon settler Isaac Behunin who is credited with naming his homestead "Little Zion" because it seemed to him to be a bit of heaven on earth.

In the 1870s, Major John Wesley Powell explored the area, describing Angels Landing, Court of the Patriarchs, and some of the park's other now-famous landmarks in his journals. At about the same time, surveyor G. K. Gilbert was mapping southern Utah. He named the Narrows and described it as "the most wonderful defile it has been my fortune to behold."

Today, Zion National Park casts a spell over you as you gaze upon its sheer multicolored walls of sandstone, explore its narrow canyons, search for hanging gardens of ferns and wildflowers, and listen to the roar of the churning, tumbling Virgin River.

A LOOK AT BRYCE CANYON

One of America's most scenic destinations, Bryce Canyon National Park is a magical land, a place of inspiration and spectacular beauty where thousands of intricately shaped rock formations stir the imagination as they stand silent watch in their colorful cathedrals. Bryce Canyon is also one of the West's most accessible national parks. Several trails lead down into the canyon—technically what geologists call an amphitheater—making it relatively easy to get to know this beautiful jewel up close. In addition, there's an easy Rim Trail, part of which is wheelchair accessible, which makes many of the park's best views available to virtually everyone.

The canyon ranges in elevation from 6,620 to 9,115 feet, with desert terrain of piñon, juniper, sagebrush, and cactus at the lower levels, and a cool high country, consisting of a dense forest of fir, spruce, and even ancient bristlecone pines. In between, where the campgrounds and visitor center are located, is a ponderosa pine forest.

Bryce Canyon is best known for its hoodoos, which geologists tell us are simply pinnacles of rock, often oddly shaped, left standing after millions of years of water and wind erosion. But perhaps a more interesting explanation lies in a Paiute legend. These American Indians, who lived in the area for several hundred years before being forced out by Anglo pioneers, told of a "Legend People" who lived here in the old days. The powerful Coyote turned them to stone for their evil ways, and today they remain frozen in time.

Whatever the cause, Bryce Canyon is delightfully unique. Its intricate and often whimsical formations are smaller and on a more human scale than the impressive rocks seen at nearby Zion. And, Bryce Canyon is far easier to explore than the sometimes intimidating vastness of Grand Canyon National Park. Bryce is comfortable

> **Impressions**
>
> *Such glorious tints, such keen contrasts of light and shade . . . can never be forgotten. . . . This is one of the grand panoramas of the plateau country.*
>
> —Geologist Clarence Dutton, 1880

and inviting in its beauty; we feel we know it simply by gazing over the rim, and we're on intimate terms after just one morning on the trail.

Although the colorful hoodoos are the first things that grab your attention, it isn't long before you notice the deep amphitheaters that envelope them, with their cliffs, windows, and arches all colored in shades of red, brown, orange, yellow, and white that change and glow with the rising and setting sun. Beyond the rocks and light are the other faces of the park: three separate life zones, each with its own unique vegetation, changing with elevation; and a kingdom of animals, from the busy chipmunks and ground squirrels to stately mule deer and their archenemy, the mountain lion. Also sometimes present in the more remote areas of the park are elk and pronghorn.

It's not known if prehistoric peoples actually saw the wonderful hoodoos at Bryce Canyon, although archaeologists do know that Paleo-Indians hunted in the area some 15,000 years ago. By about A.D. 700, the Basket Makers had established small villages in Paria Valley, east of Bryce Canyon in what is now Grand Staircase–Escalante National Monument, also discussed in this book. (See chapter 9.) By about A.D. 1100, Ancestral Puebloan peoples (also called the Anasazi) were living east of Bryce Canyon, and are believed to have visited what is now the park, in search of game and timber.

However, serious exploration of the Bryce area likely began later, with the Paiutes; and it's possible that trappers, prospectors, and early Mormon scouts may have visited here in the early to mid-1800s before Major John Wesley Powell conducted the first thorough survey of the region in the early 1870s. Shortly after Powell's exploration of the park area—in 1875—Mormon pioneer Ebenezer Bryce, a Scottish carpenter, and his wife, Mary, moved here and tried raising cattle. Their home became known as "Bryce's Canyon." Although they stayed only 5 years before moving to Arizona, Bryce's legacy is his name and his oft-quoted description of the canyon as "a helluva place to lose a cow."

The smallest of Utah's five national parks, with an area of just under 36,000 acres, Bryce Canyon was declared a national monument by President Warren Harding in 1923. The following year, Congress passed provisional legislation to make this area into "Utah National Park." In 1928, the change in status was finalized and the park was renamed Bryce Canyon National Park, in honor of one of its early residents.

EXPLORING ZION NATIONAL PARK

Utah's first and most popular national park, Zion is a spectacularly beautiful spot that offers a wide variety of sights and experiences. The park is home to creatures of practically all shapes and sizes, from the minute Zion snail—almost too small to see at all—on up. Massive rock formations, such as the Great White Throne, give one the feeling that this land is something permanent, but the beautiful Narrows, where time and water have carved huge chunks of stone into a delicate work of art, prove otherwise.

ESSENTIALS

ACCESS/ENTRY POINTS Zion National Park has two main sections: **Zion Canyon,** the main part of the park, and the less-visited **Kolob Canyons.** The main east-west road through Zion Canyon is the park-owned extension of Utah 9; from this road, the park's 12-mile round-trip Zion Canyon Scenic Drive heads north, providing access to most of the scenic overlooks and trail heads.

Utah 9 connects to both sides of Zion National Park, giving the main section of the park two entry gates— south and east. The south entrance, at Springdale, is by far the more popular, with two-thirds of park visitors arriving there. Most area lodgings and restaurants are found in Springdale. (See chapter 4, "Where to Stay, Camp & Eat in Zion.") In addition, the park's two campgrounds and the Zion Canyon Visitor Center are located just inside the south entrance.

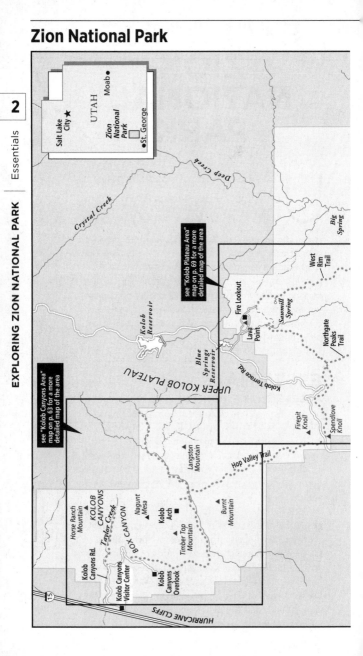

see "Kolob Plateau Area" map on p. 69 for a more detailed map of the area

see "Kolob Canyons Area" map on p. 63 for a more detailed map of the area

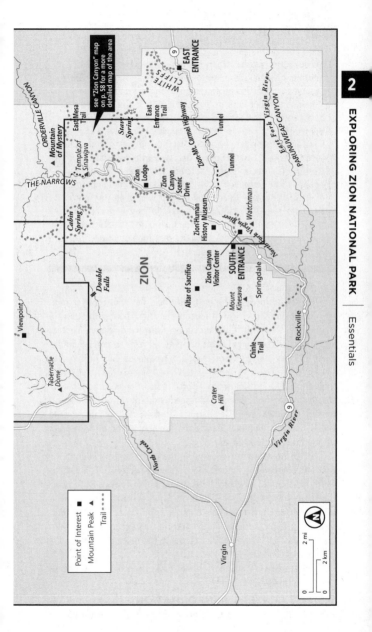

see "Zion Canyon" map on p. 58 for a more detailed map of the area

EAST ENTRANCE

WHITE CLIFFS

ORDERVILLE CANYON

▲ Mountain of Mystery

East Mesa Trail

Staav Spring

East Entrance Trail

Temple of Sinawava

THE NARROWS

Zion Lodge

Zion Canyon Scenic Drive

Zion–Mt. Carmel Highway

Tunnel

Tunnel

Cabin Spring

Zion-Human History Museum

Watchman

North Fork Virgin River

East Fork Virgin River

PARUNUWEAP CANYON

Double Falls

ZION

Altar of Sacrifice

Zion Canyon Visitor Center

SOUTH ENTRANCE

Mount Kinesava

Springdale

Chinle Trail

Rockville

Viewpoint

Tabernacle Dome

Crater Hill

North Creek

Virgin River

9

Virgin

Point of Interest ■
Mountain Peak ▲
Trail ·····

0   2 mi
0   2 km

WHERE TO FIND restrooms IN ZION

The all-important restrooms at Zion are generally well maintained, but vary considerably in the facilities they offer. As at most national parks, the best restrooms are at the visitor centers, where you'll find heated rooms with sinks and flush toilets. There are also public restrooms at the Zion Lodge shuttle stop. South and Watchman campgrounds, the Grotto Picnic Area, the Human History Museum, and the Temple of Sinawava Trail Head have sinks and flush toilets. Lava Point Campground, Kolob Canyons Viewpoint, Scout Lookout, and Weeping Rock and Canyon Overlook trail heads have vault toilets. Although essentially outhouses, this type of facility has come a long way in the past 25 or 30 years—they're clean, sanitary, and, best of all, they don't smell. However, they lack lights, water for hand washing, and heat. There are no toilets along the trails or in the backcountry.

During busy times, some facilities may run out of toilet paper, so it's best to carry a backup supply.

There is no town at the east entrance, but that route is more scenic—it drops over 2,500 feet in elevation, passes through the 1-mile-long Zion–Mt. Carmel Tunnel, and winds down six steep switchbacks. The tunnel is off limits to bicycles. It can accommodate two-way traffic when standard passenger cars and pickup trucks are being used, but it is too small for two-way traffic that includes larger vehicles, so opposite-direction traffic must be stopped when motor homes, campers, and other larger vehicles are passing through (see "Regulations," below). Those also visiting Bryce Canyon National Park will probably enter or leave Zion through the east entrance.

The **Kolob Canyons** section, in the park's northwest corner, is easily reached on the short Kolob Canyons Road off I-15, at exit 40.

About 15 miles west of Zion Canyon, Kolob Terrace Road heads north from the village of Virgin off Utah 9, providing access to several backcountry trails (see chapter 3, "Hikes & Other Outdoor Pursuits in Zion National Park") and the Lava Point Campground (see chapter 5, "Where to Stay, Camp & Eat in Zion"). This road is closed in the winter.

To get to Bryce Canyon National Park, head north and east on Utah 9, U.S. 89, and Utah 12.

VISITOR CENTERS & INFORMATION The park has two visitor centers. The **Zion Canyon Visitor Center,** near the south entrance to the park, has a wide variety of outdoor exhibits. Rangers answer questions and provide backcountry permits; free brochures are available; and books, maps, videos, postcards, and posters are sold. In summer, it is open daily from 8am to 7:30pm, with shorter hours the rest of the year. The **Kolob Canyons Visitor Center,** in the northwest corner of the park, right off I-15, provides information, permits, books, and maps. It is open from 8am to 6pm in summer, with shorter hours the rest of the year.

The **Zion Human History Museum,** located about 1 mile inside the south entrance, offers museum exhibits, park information, and an orientation program, plus a bookstore. It's open daily in summer from 9am to 7pm, with shorter hours at other times.

Both visitor centers and the museum are closed on Christmas Day.

FEES   Entry into the park (for up to 7 days), which includes unlimited use of the shuttle bus, costs $25 per private vehicle (car, pickup truck, van, or RV); $12 per individual ages 16 or older on motorcycle, bicycle, or foot. Oversize vehicles are charged $15 for use of the Zion–Mt. Carmel Tunnel on the east side of the park (see "Regulations," below).

Backcountry permits, available at either visitor center, are required for all overnight hikes in the park as well as for any slot canyon hikes. Permits cost $10 for 1 or 2 people, $15 for 3 to 7, and $20 for 8 to 12 people. Camping in Watchman and South campgrounds costs $16 per night for basic campsites and $18 to $20 per night for sites with electric hookups (located in Watchman Campground); campsites in the small, primitive Lava Point Campground are free.

REGULATIONS   The 1-mile-long Zion–Mt. Carmel Tunnel is too small for two-way traffic that includes vehicles larger than standard passenger cars and pickup trucks. (See "Historic & Man-Made Attractions," later in this chapter.) All vehicles over 7'10" wide (including mirrors) or 11'4" tall (including luggage racks and so forth) must be driven down the center of the tunnel, and therefore all traffic from the opposite direction must be stopped. These oversize vehicles must pay a $15 fee, which is good for two trips through the tunnel during a 7-day period. Drivers pay the fee at the entrance stations. All vehicles over 13'1" tall and other particularly large vehicles are prohibited from driving anywhere on the park road between the east entrance and Zion Canyon. Call the park headquarters if you have questions about accessibility for your vehicle.

Bicycles are prohibited in the Zion–Mt. Carmel Tunnel, the backcountry, and on trails, except the Pa'rus Trail. Feeding or disturbing wildlife is forbidden, as is vandalism and disturbing any natural feature of the park. Pets, which must be leashed at all times, are prohibited on all trails (except the Pa'rus Trail, where leashed pets are permitted), in the backcountry, in public buildings, and on the shuttles.

Backcountry hikers should practice minimum impact techniques and are prohibited from building fires. A limit on the number of people allowed in various parts of the backcountry may be in force during your visit; prospective backcountry hikers should check with rangers before setting out. You can purchase a backcountry permit at the visitor center the day before or the day of your trip, and reservations for permits can be made in advance through the park's website, www.nps.gov/zion, although they must still be picked up in person at the visitor center.

TIPS FROM A PARK RANGER

"One of the most spectacular places on earth," is how Ron Terry, Zion National Park's former chief of interpretation, describes the park. "Its beauty and grandeur are overpowering. You cannot visit Zion without being inspired and awestruck by the immensity of the towering sandstone cliffs and deep, narrow canyons."

However, even though Zion is the most visited national park in Utah, Terry says it is still possible to find solitude in its numerous out-of-the-way places.

"One of Zion's lesser-known but stunningly beautiful areas is Kolob Canyons," Terry says. "The Kolob Canyons Scenic Drive includes numerous pullouts, providing a chance to get out of the car and drink in the beauty of the red sandstone cliffs and hanging valleys of the Finger Canyons of the Kolob."

"The hike up the Middle Fork of Taylor Creek to Double Arch Alcove is well worth the trip, as is the more strenuous hike to Kolob Arch," Terry says. He advises that visitors should be sure to stop first at the Kolob Canyon Visitor Center for current hiking information.

"If you visit Zion in March, April, October, or November you will be sharing the park with fewer people and still have access to most of the park's trails," Terry says. "October and November are particularly beautiful," he adds. "The yellow and gold leaves of the trees along the Virgin River and in its side canyons contrast wonderfully with the reddish colored sandstone of the canyon walls."

According to Terry, your first stop in the park should be at a visitor center to get current weather and flash-flood-potential information, purchase any needed backcountry permits, and get advice from rangers on which trails and attractions are best for you.

Attending one of the park's ranger naturalist programs will also enhance your park experience, according to Terry, who adds, "The time spent attending one of these programs is time well spent." During warmer months there are nightly programs in the campgrounds and at Zion Lodge; plus there are daily talks and ranger-guided shuttle tours.

Terry also suggests a visit to the Zion Human History Museum, which opened in 2002 and features exhibits on how humans have interacted with the geology, water, plants, and animals of the park. An informative orientation film is shown in the museum auditorium.

Although the vast majority of Zion's visitors have a thoroughly enjoyable experience with no serious problems, the park does have some very serious potential dangers.

The Narrows hike, in which hikers spend most of their time in the water, is one of the most popular hikes in the park, but also one of the most potentially dangerous, according to Terry. Before attempting this or any hike in a narrow canyon, visitors need to check at the visitor center for weather forecasts and flash-flood potential, he says.

"Cold and swift water, slippery and uneven walking surfaces, potential flash flooding, and potential hypothermia are all factors to be considered when planning for this hike," Terry says. "Good footwear with ankle support is a must. A walking stick will make the experience much more enjoyable."

Also very popular at Zion are canyoneering and rock climbing. "Canyoneering is a strenuous activity involving traversing narrow slot canyons, usually requiring rappelling equipment and skills," Terry says, and "climbing the towering vertical cliffs in the park is a high-risk activity that should only be attempted by expert climbers."

The soft sandstone of Zion's cliffs and the prohibition of drilling into the rock make climbing in the park doubly dangerous, according to Terry, and climbers who are not experts should obtain their experience in other less extreme conditions.

"Zion is in a desert environment and the summer sun can be very hot," Terry says. "Whatever activity you are participating in should include carrying and drinking plenty of water. Hats and sunscreen are also a must. Know your limits and don't be afraid to end an activity and return another day."

THE HIGHLIGHTS

There is such a wide variety of things to do and see, but probably the single most important activity for visitors is traveling the **Zion Canyon Scenic Drive** ★★ (by shuttle bus from April through

How to Snap Great Wildlife Photos

The key to getting good wildlife photos is to know the animals' habits, such as where they go and when. Then, get there first and quietly wait.

October, your car the rest of the year), stopping at viewpoints to see many of the park's best-known rock formations.

Among the spectacular rock formations that you won't want to miss is the **Great White Throne ★★★**, which can be seen from Zion Canyon Scenic Drive as well as from several hiking trails, including Observation Point Trail, Deertrap Mountain Trail, Angels Landing Trail, and Emerald Pools Trail. (See chapter 3, "Hikes & Other Outdoor Pursuits in Zion National Park.") Considered the symbol of Zion National Park for many visitors, this massive and imposing block of Navajo sandstone towers 2,000 feet above the North Fork of the Virgin River. It can be especially impressive when colored by the setting sun. A postage stamp depicting the Great White Throne was issued in the 1930s.

Another eye-catcher is the huge **Checkerboard Mesa,** which you pass when entering the park from the east. This huge dome of sandstone has a fishnet pattern created by a unique form of erosion and weathering. Although horizontal lines in Navajo sandstone are fairly common, experts believe that the rare vertical lines were formed by freezing and thawing processes, and then enlarged by running water. For more information on the mesa, see "Seeing the Park by Car and Shuttle," below.

Those who think of southern Utah as nothing but burning desert will learn differently at **Weeping Rock,** a short but steep walk along Weeping Rock Trail. Its name comes from the spring water that continually runs down the vertical face of the rock, nurturing hanging gardens. For more information on this feature, see chapter 3, "Hikes & Other Outdoor Pursuits in Zion National Parks," and chapter 9, "A Nature Guide to Zion & Bryce Canyon National Parks."

The **Emerald Pools ★★** provide another look at the wet side of Zion—lush green plants, pretty pools of water, and two delightful cascading waterfalls. In a short canyon near Zion Lodge, the lower pool is an easy walk along a paved path, while the two upper pools require a bit of real hiking. The pools' rich green color is the result of algae in the water. For more information, see p. 37.

At the end of the Zion Canyon Scenic Drive is the **Temple of Sinawava,** a picturesque canyon surrounded by rock walls reaching

WILDLIFE VIEWING & bird-watching

It's a rare visitor to Zion who doesn't spot a critter of some sort, from **mule deer**—often observed along roadways and in campgrounds year-round—to the numerous varieties of lizards seen from spring through fall, including the park's largest lizard, the **chuckwalla,** which can grow to 20 inches long. There has been an increasing number of sightings of **desert Bighorn sheep** and even an occasional **mountain lion** along Utah 9 (the Zion–Mt. Carmel Hwy.), on the east side of the park. Along the Virgin River, you'll see **bank beaver,** so named because they live in burrows dug into riverbanks instead of dams.

If you're interested in spotting birds, you're in luck at Zion. The **peregrine falcon,** among the world's fastest birds, is sometimes seen along the Angels Landing and Cable Mountain trails and in the area of the Great White Throne. It sometimes nests in the Weeping Rock area, where you're also likely to see the American dipper, canyon wren, and white-throated swift. **Bald eagles** sometimes winter in the park, and you might also see golden eagles. **Red-tailed hawks** are fairly common, as are great blue herons, American kestrels, Gambel's quail, mourning doves, great horned owls, western kingbirds, common ravens, piñon jays, Steller's Jays, yellow-rumped warblers, wild turkeys, and American robins.

Snakes include the poisonous **Great Basin rattlesnake,** found below 8,000 feet elevation; there are also nonpoisonous king snakes and gopher snakes. Amphibians found in the park include the Arizona tiger salamander, Great Basin spadefoot, red-spotted toad, and northern leopard frog. **Tarantulas,** those large, usually slow-moving hairy spiders, are often seen in late summer and fall. Although the tarantula's bite is not significantly poisonous to most people, it may be somewhat painful.

Remember, it's illegal to feed the wildlife. It's not healthy for the wildlife to eat human food or to get used to being fed this way. For additional details on the wildlife at Zion, see chapter 9, "A Nature Guide to Zion & Bryce Canyon National Parks."

2,000 feet into the sky. Here, you'll discover the aptly named Pulpit and Altar rock formations, as well as maple and cottonwood trees and a spectacular waterfall that cascades almost 1,000 feet down the temple's west wall during the spring and summer. This is the beginning of the Riverside Walk, discussed below and on p. 38.

The **Riverside Walk** ★★★, one of the park's easiest trails, should not be ignored just because it's not a challenge. It begins at the Temple of Sinawava and parallels the Virgin River, providing a good sense of the steepness of the canyon walls as you approach the Narrows. Along the walk are interpretive signs discussing this particular ecosystem. This is a good place to hear, and possibly see, the canyon tree frog, plus the American dipper and other park wildlife. For more information see p. 38, in chapter 3, "Hikes & Other Outdoor Pursuits in Zion National Park"; also see chapter 9, "A Nature Guide to Zion & Bryce Canyon National Parks."

For a unique hiking experience as well as a close-up look at the power of water, venture into the **Narrows ★★★**, a section of the Virgin River, where the canyon walls are less than 30 feet apart in spots but stand over 1,000 feet tall. To travel between these delicately sculpted rock walls, you'll hike and wade. The Narrows can be experienced as a short day hike, a long 1-day through-hike, or an overnight hike—although caution is needed because the Narrows is prone to flash flooding. For details, see p. 48, in chapter 3, "Hikes & Other Outdoor Pursuits in Zion National Park"; also see chapter 9, "A Nature Guide to Zion & Bryce Canyon National Parks."

An often-overlooked area of Zion National Park is the **Kolob Canyons** section, in the park's northwest corner. With its narrow canyons and brightly colored cliffs, this is a somewhat different world than Zion Canyon. There's a scenic drive with spectacular overlooks, and several hiking trails. See the section "Seeing the Park by Car and Shuttle," below, as well as p. 48.

SEEING THE PARK IN 1 OR 2 DAYS

The best way to see Zion is to spend a week in the park, starting with the visitor center displays and programs, then taking a Zion Canyon Scenic Drive trip on the shuttle bus, and gradually working from short hikes and walks to full-day and overnight treks into the backcountry.

If you have only a day or two, we recommend that your first stop be the **Zion Canyon Visitor Center,** near the south entrance to the park, to see the exhibits; look through the free *Zion Map & Guide,* which describes various hiking and viewing options; and finally talk with a ranger about the amount of time you have, your abilities, and your interests.

If your goal is to see as much of the park as possible in 1 full day, we suggest the following:

After a quick stop at the visitor center, hop on the shuttle bus, which hits the major Zion Canyon roadside viewpoints, plus the

Zion Human History Museum. When you get to the **Temple of Sinawava** (p. 24), instead of just taking a quick look and jumping on the next shuttle, hike the easy 2-mile round-trip **Riverside Walk** (p. 38), which follows the Virgin River through a narrow canyon past hanging gardens. Then continue the shuttle bus trek back to the lodge (total time: 2–4 hr.), where you might stop at the gift shop and possibly have lunch in the lodge restaurant.

Near the lodge, you'll find the trail head for the **Emerald Pools** (p. 37). Especially pleasant on hot days, this easy walk through a forest of oak, maple, fir, and cottonwood trees leads to a waterfall, hanging garden, and the shimmering lower pool of the Emerald Pools. This part of the walk should take about an hour round-trip; those with a bit more ambition may want to add another hour and another mile to the loop by taking the moderately strenuous hike on a rocky, steeper trail to the upper pool.

If you still have time and energy, drive back toward the south park entrance and stop at **Watchman Trail Head** (p. 40). Here, a moderately strenuous, 2-mile, 2-hour round-trip hike takes you to a plateau with beautiful views of several rock formations and the town of Springdale. That evening, try to take in the campground amphitheater program.

SEEING THE PARK BY CAR & SHUTTLE

If you enter the park from the east, along the steep **Zion–Mt. Carmel Highway,** you'll travel 13 miles to the **Zion Canyon Visitor Center,** passing between the White Cliffs and Checkerboard Mesa, a massive sandstone rock formation covered with horizontal and vertical lines that make it look like a huge fishing net. Continuing, you'll pass through a fairyland of fantastically shaped rocks of red, orange, tan, and white, as well as the **Great Arch of Zion,** carved by the forces of erosion high in a stone cliff. At the east end of the Zion–Mt. Carmel Tunnel is the **trail head parking** for the Canyon Overlook Trail, a relatively easy 1-mile walk to a great viewpoint (p. 36). After driving through the tunnel, you'll traverse a number of long switchbacks as you descend to the canyon floor. (See "Regulations," under "Essentials," earlier in this chapter, for information on getting through the tunnel.)

The park's shuttle bus system consists of two loops: One in the town of Springdale and the other along Zion Canyon Scenic Drive, with the loops connecting at the transit/visitor center just inside the south park entrance. April through October, access to Zion

Wildlife Viewing

The earlier in the day you can get out on the Zion Canyon Scenic Drive, the better chance you'll have of seeing wildlife.

Canyon Scenic Drive (above Utah 9) is limited to shuttle buses, hikers, and bikers. The only exception will be overnight Zion Lodge guests and tour buses connected with the lodge, which will have access to the road as far as the lodge. Shuttle stops are located at all the major-use areas in the park, and shuttles run frequently (about every 6 min. at peak times). In winter, when visitation is lowest in the park, visitors are permitted to drive the full length of Zion Canyon Scenic Drive in their own vehicles. Complete information about the shuttle and all stops is available at the visitor center.

The ride through Zion Canyon is impressive by any standards, with massive stone reaching straight up to the heavens, and the North Fork of the Virgin River threading its way through the maze of rocks. In every direction, the views are awe-inspiring. Pullouts along the road provide access to viewpoints and hiking trails. (See chapter 3, "Hikes & Other Outdoor Pursuits in Zion National Park.")

The first pullout is across from the **Court of the Patriarchs,** where a short paved trail leads to an impressive viewpoint. The next stop is **Zion Lodge** (p. 55), and across the road from the lodge is the trail head for the **Emerald Pools trail system.** The Grotto Picnic Area is about a half mile beyond the lodge, and a trail, paralleling Zion Canyon Scenic Drive, leads from the lodge to the picnic area. Across from the Grotto Picnic Area parking lot is a footbridge that leads to the Emerald Pools, Angels Landing, and West Rim trails.

Continuing north into Zion Canyon, the road passes the **Great White Throne** on the right and then **Angels Landing** on the left, before the turnoff to the **Weeping Rock Trail Head** parking area. From here the road closely traces the curves of the river, with a couple of stops to allow different views of the **Organ,** which to some resembles a huge pipe organ. Finally, the road ends at the **Temple of Sinawava,** where the paved **Riverside Walk** follows the Virgin River toward the **Narrows,** one of the most incredible sights in Zion.

To escape the crowds of Zion Canyon, head to the northwest corner of the park. The **Kolob Canyons Road** (about 45 min.

from Zion Canyon Visitor Center, at exit 40 of I-15) runs 5 miles among spectacular red and orange rocks, ending at a high vista. Allow about 45 minutes round-trip, including stops at numbered viewpoints. Here's what you'll pass along the way:

Leaving **Kolob Canyons Visitor Center,** drive along the Hurricane Fault to **Hurricane Cliffs,** a series of tall, gray cliffs composed of limestone, and onward to **Taylor Creek,** where a piñon-juniper forest clings to life on the rocky hillside, providing a home to the bright blue scrub jay. Your next stop is **Horse Ranch Mountain,** which, at 8,726 feet, is the park's highest point. Passing a series of colorful rock layers, where you might be lucky enough to spot a golden eagle, your next stop is **Box Canyon,** along the South Fork of Taylor Creek, with sheer rock walls soaring over 1,500 feet high. Along this stretch are multicolored layers of rock, pushed upward by tremendous forces within the earth, followed by a side canyon, with large arched alcoves with delicate curved ceilings. Head on to a view of **Timber Top Mountain,** which has a sagebrush-blanketed desert at its base, but is covered with stately fir and ponderosa pine at its peak. Watch for mule deer on the brushy hillsides, especially between October and March, around sunrise or sunset. Continue to **Rockfall Overlook,** where a large scar on the mountainside marks the spot where a 1,000-foot chunk of stone crashed to the earth in July 1983 from erosion. Finally, stop to see the canyon walls themselves, colored orange-red by iron oxide and striped black by mineral-laden water running down the cliff faces.

Probably the least visited area is between Zion Canyon and Kolob Canyons, accessible via the **Kolob Terrace Road** (also called the Kolob Rd.). Heading north off Utah 9 from the village of Virgin, about 15 miles west of the park's southern entrance, the Kolob Terrace Road climbs through piñon-juniper woodlands, past grassy meadows, and up into a forest of ponderosa pines and aspen. There's a viewpoint offering panoramic vistas, a picnic area, vault toilets, and the small Lava Point Campground. Views from the road are most dramatic coming down. This road is closed in the winter.

HISTORIC & MAN-MADE ATTRACTIONS

There are no major historic sites at Zion National Park, but there is some archaeological evidence of the early peoples who inhabited the area, plus a few 20th-century structures of historic interest.

Archaeologists have found evidence of several historic and prehistoric cultures throughout the park. It is believed that people from the **Archaic Period** occupied the area from about 7,000 to 2,500 years ago; it is thought that people of the **Virgin Anasazi Pueblo culture** lived at Zion until about A.D. 1150; and the **Southern Paiutes,** who arrived in the area at about A.D. 1100, stayed in the area until European settlers arrived in about 1860. Although there are few designated and marked archaeological sites, hikers with sharp eyes may see pot shards, pieces of ancient stone tools, rock art, and other artifacts. There's a site with rock art near the park's south entrance; ask rangers for specific directions. **Refrain from touching** these artifacts—especially rock art and painted pottery, because skin oils can damage them.

Just outside the Zion Canyon Visitor Center, the short but steep **Archeology Trail** (.4 mile round-trip with an 80-foot elevation gain), leads to the outlines of small prehistoric storage buildings. There are also some trailside exhibits and interpretive signs.

From the **Weeping Rock** parking area, you can see remains of a **cable operation** that was used to lower millions of board feet of timber from Cable Mountain to the floor of Zion Canyon between 1901 and 1926. (See section 1, "Day Hikes," in chapter 3.) The timber was used to build pioneer settlements along the Virgin River.

Along **Taylor Creek** in the Kolob Canyons section of the park are the remains of two cabins. The **Gustav Larson homestead cabin,** built in 1930 of white fir logs brought from Cedar City, is near the confluence of the North and Middle forks. Arthur Fife, a teacher at Branch Agricultural College (now Southern Utah University), also built a **homestead cabin** of white fir logs in 1930. This cabin is perched above the north bank of the creek. (See "Middle Fork of Taylor Creek" in chapter 3.)

Also from that period is the **Zion–Mt. Carmel Tunnel,** which you'll drive through if you're entering or leaving the park on the east side. Dedicated on July 4, 1930, the 1-mile tunnel cost over $500,000 and took longer than 3 years to build. At the time it opened, it was the longest tunnel in the United States. Another historic structure, the handsome **Zion Lodge,** was built in 1925 by the Union Pacific Railroad, but was destroyed by fire in 1966. It was rebuilt the following year and restored to its historic appearance in 1991. Several 1920s-era restored **tourist cabins** are located near the lodge.

The park's **Zion Human History Museum,** 1 mile inside the south entrance, has exhibits on human interaction with the geology, water, plants, and animals of the park. An informative orientation film is shown in the museum auditorium. The museum is open daily in summer from 9am to 7pm, with shorter hours at other times.

RANGER & EDUCATIONAL PROGRAMS

Zion National Park has some of the best **ranger programs ★★** we have encountered, and even better, they're all free. **Evening programs,** which last about 45 minutes, take place at the Watchman Campground Amphitheater and at the Zion Lodge Auditorium. They usually include a slide show, take place most evenings from April through September, and include topics such as the animals or plants of the park, geology, the night sky, mankind's role in the park, or some unique aspect of Zion, such as slot canyons. Rangers also give **short talks** during the day at various locations, including the Zion Lodge Auditorium and the Zion Human History Museum. Ranger-guided **hikes and walks,** which may require reservations, might take you to little-visited areas of the park, on a trek to see wildflowers, or for a night hike under a full moon. These range from easy to very difficult. When the shuttle is operating, the 2-hour **Ride with a Ranger** trip offers an opportunity to see the scenic drive, and learn about Zion Canyon, from a park ranger's perspective. Reservations can be made up to one day in advance at the visitor center.

Schedules of the various programs and activities are posted on bulletin boards at the visitor centers and campgrounds.

The **Zion Canyon Field Institute,** operated by the nonprofit Zion Natural History Association, Zion National Park, Springdale, UT 84767 (✆ **800/635-3959,** 435/772-3265, or 435/772-3264 for the Field Institute; www.zionpar.org), offers a variety of single and multiday outdoor workshops and classes, covering subjects in the sciences, arts, and humanities. Programs take place year-round in Zion National Park and nearby Cedar Breaks National Monument. (See chapter 8, "Nearby Things to See & Do.") Recent program titles have included Bird Watching, Hanging Gardens of Zion, Wasps & Ants, Bat Biology & Conservation, Zion by Moonlight, Fall Foliage Photo Workshop, Zion Narrows, Watercolor Journaling, and Winter

Photography. Although all the Field Institute's programs are very rewarding, we especially recommend the **photo workshops ★★**, which are led by institute director Michael Plyler, an excellent photographer and teacher. Fees for most of the 1-day programs range from $35 to $300. Most have a minimum age of 15 or 16. Members of the **Zion Natural History Association** (p. 174) receive a 20% discount on most Zion Canyon Field Institute programs.

GUIDED TOURS

Guided **horseback rides** in the park are available from **Canyon Trail Rides;** and guided biking, hiking, and rock climbing trips, both within and outside the park, are offered by **Zion Adventure Company** and **Zion Rock & Mountain Guides.** See chapter 3, "Hikes & Other Outdoor Pursuits in Zion National Park."

Although we highly recommend the local companies mentioned above, those who prefer major national companies will find that several **national tour operators** offer guided trips as well; see "Package & Adventure Tours" in chapter 10, "Planning Your Trip to Zion & Bryce Canyon National Parks."

ESPECIALLY FOR KIDS

One of the nicest things about Zion National Park is the wide variety of hiking trails that it offers—there is usually a path suited to every family member's interest and ability level. Among trails that children find especially enjoyable are the **Weeping Rock Trail,** because it leads to a fascinating rock that oozes water; and the various **Emerald Pools trails,** which take you to a series of attractive little pools, where you just might see—or at least hear—some frogs. The only problem at the Emerald Pools is that kids (and adults, too) have to resist the strong urge to submerge their toes in the dark green water (swimming is not permitted).

Older youths—perhaps young teens—who are in good physical condition will enjoy hiking into the **Narrows** from the end of the Riverside Walk, where a hike is almost a swim, and you're staring up from the bottom of a 1,000-foot ravine. However, the Narrows

---

😄 Kidding Around

Kids love the huge screen and dramatic photography in the *Zion Canyon: Treasure of the Gods* production at the **Zion Canyon Theatre.** See chapter 8, "Nearby Things to See & Do."

can be very hazardous, so discuss plans with park rangers in advance. See chapter 3, "Hikes & Other Outdoor Pursuits in Zion National Park," for more hiking information.

Park rangers also run special programs just for children. Kids 11 and under can join the **Junior Rangers/Explorers** ★★ and participate in a variety of hands-on activities, earning certificates, pins, and patches. Morning and afternoon sessions, each lasting 1½ to 2½ hours, take place daily from Memorial Day through Labor Day, with children meeting at the Zion Nature Center, near the entrance to South Campground.

HIKES & OTHER OUTDOOR PURSUITS IN ZION NATIONAL PARK

Zion offers a wide variety of hiking trails and opportunities, ranging from easy half-hour walks to grueling overnight hikes. Brochures and books on hiking trails are available at the visitor centers, and current information is also in the official Zion Map and Guide. Hikers with a fear of heights should be especially careful when choosing trails—many, such as the Angels Landing Trail, include steep, dizzying drop-offs. The authors and other experienced hikers provide ratings, but these are entirely subjective.

Guided hiking, rock climbing, and biking trips in the park and surrounding area are offered by several reliable local companies, including **Zion Adventure Company,** 36 Lion Blvd., at the corner of Lion Boulevard and Zion Park Boulevard (P.O. Box 523), Springdale, UT 84767 (**© 435/772-1001;** www.zionadvertures. com); and **Zion Rock & Mountain Guides,** 1458 Zion Park Blvd. (P.O. Box 623), Springdale, UT 84767 (**© 435/772-3303;** www.zionrockguides.com). **Zion Cycles,** 868 Zion Park Blvd., behind Zion Pizza & Noodle (P.O. Box 624), Springdale, UT 84767 (**© 435/ 772-0400;** www.zioncycles.com), rents, repairs, and advises about mountain and road bikes. National companies offering guided hiking/biking trips in the area are discussed on p. 162.

In the park, the free shuttle usually offers the best way for hikers to reach trail heads, and each shuttle has racks for two bikes. Zion Adventure Company and Zion Rock & Mountain Guides (see above) also provide shuttle services.

DAY HIKES

Hikers have the chance to see the park from two completely different perspectives—a high plateau hike affords a look down into the canyons, while a descent into the canyons provides spectacular views skyward. See chapter 2 for more information on the different areas and highlights of the park.

Note: "RT" stands for round-trip in the following trail listings.

Shorter Hikes

Riverside Walk (with assistance) and Pa'rus Trail are the only trails that are wheelchair accessible.

Angels Landing Trail ★★   A popular though strenuous hike that is most certainly not for anyone with even a mild fear of heights, this trail climbs 1,488 feet to a summit that offers spectacular views into Zion Canyon. **Be prepared:** The final half-mile follows a narrow, knife-edge trail along a steep ridge, where footing can be slippery even under the best of circumstances.

After crossing the footbridge over the Virgin River, turn north through a riparian woodland of cottonwood, box elder, and tamarisk, beneath Angels Landing. The trail climbs to the mouth of Refrigerator Canyon, around the west side of the monolith. Grottos and overhangs dot the red sandstone canyon walls.

Right before the head of the canyon, the series of 21 switchbacks built into a cleft in the wall is regarded as one of the engineering marvels of the park. At the top of the switchbacks, you begin the gradual ascent to Scout Lookout, the saddle behind Angels Landing, from which you get spectacular views into Zion Canyon. Here, the West Rim Trail heads off to the left, while the Angels Landing Trail turns southeast and begins the final brutal climb along the spine of a razorlike ridge. From this point, many stretches have support chains to hold on to, though there are no guardrails on Angels Landing itself. The views are stupendous, with the Virgin River gently bending around three sides at the bottom of the canyon, the Great White Throne and Red Arch Mountain to the southeast, and the entrance to the Narrows beyond the Temple of Sinawava to the north. See map on p. 36.

5.4 miles RT. Difficult. Access: Grotto Picnic Area along Zion Canyon Scenic Dr.

Zion Canyon

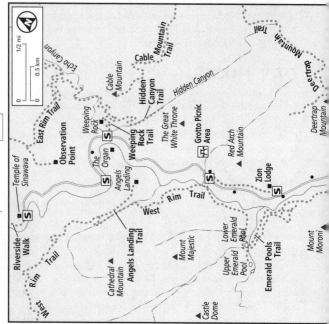

Canyon Overlook Trail   Panoramic vistas are the lure on this self-guided trail that takes you to an overlook offering a magnificent view of lower Zion Canyon, the East and West temples, the Towers of the Virgin, and the Streaked Wall. The trail, which is sometimes slippery because of sand, begins with a series of uneven steps cut into the sandstone. There are long drop-offs into the narrow chasm of Pine Creek Canyon. The hike has an elevation gain of 163 feet. See map above.

1 mile RT. Moderate. Access: Parking area at the east terminus of the Zion–Mt. Carmel Tunnel.

Court of the Patriarchs   This short, steep, paved trail leads to a viewpoint that provides vistas of the Streaked Wall and the Sentinel to the south, the Court of the Patriarchs and Mount Moroni straight ahead (west), the Spearhead and Angels Landing to the north, and Mountain of the Sun and Twin Brothers above and behind (east). A footbridge crosses the river and connects to the Sand Bench Trail. See map above.

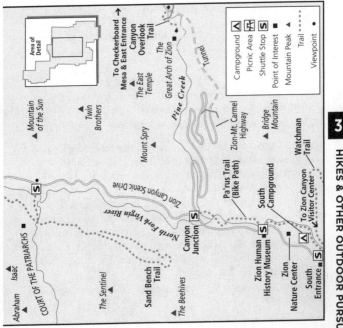

300 ft. RT. Easy. Access: Court of the Patriarchs parking area along Zion Canyon Scenic Dr.

Emerald Pools Trail System ★★ ☺ This can be either an easy 1-hour walk, if you just visit the Lower Pool, or a moderately strenuous 2-hour hike, if you decide to continue to the other pools. A .6-mile paved path leads from the Emerald Pools parking area through a forest of oak, maple, fir, and cottonwood, to several waterfalls, a hanging garden, and the picturesque Lower Emerald Pool. From here, a steeper, rocky trail continues .25 miles to Middle Emerald Pool, and then climbs another .3 mile past cactus, yucca, and juniper to Upper Emerald Pool, with another waterfall. As you climb the trail, there are views of soaring stone formations such as Lady Mountain, the Spearhead, Mount Majestic, Red Arch Mountain, Deertrap Mountain, and the Great White Throne. From the Middle Pool there is a long drop-off leading to the Lower Pool; the Upper Pool is enclosed on three sides by sheer cliffs and on the fourth by boulders. Total elevation gain is 69 feet to Lower

Emerald Pool, 150 feet to Middle Emerald Pool, and 400 feet from the trail head to Upper Emerald Pool. Swimming or wading is not permitted in any of the pools. See map on p. 36.

1.2–2.5 miles RT. Easy to moderate. Access: Trail head across from Zion Lodge.

Hidden Canyon Trail   A particularly scenic hike along a paved trail that's sometimes cut from solid stone, Hidden Canyon Trail climbs 850 feet to the mouth of a narrow water-carved canyon. You'll pass slickrock formations, or smooth wind-polished rock formations, and sheer cliffs—stay back from the edges, as they may be unstable and slippery. Walking up the dry streambed into the canyon, you'll pass grottos and other water-formed decorations on the canyon walls, including a small natural arch about a half-mile upstream. This trail is not recommended for anyone with a fear of heights. See map on p. 36.

2.4 miles RT. Moderate to difficult. Access: Weeping Rock parking lot, along Zion Canyon Scenic Dr.

Pa'rus Trail ★★ ☺   This easy, paved trail (suitable for wheelchairs and baby strollers) follows the Virgin River, crossing it several times. It provides views of the rock formations in lower Zion Canyon, including the West Temple, Watchman, Bridge Mountain, Sentinel, and East Temple formations. The trail has a 50-foot elevation gain and, unlike other park trails, is also open to bicycles (see "Biking & Mountain Biking," later in this chapter) and leashed pets. Watch for stop signs, where the trail crosses park roads, stay alert, and be aware of vehicles whose drivers may not easily see you on the winding roads. This trail links the campgrounds and south park entrance with the beginning of Zion Canyon Scenic Drive (closed to private vehicles, except in winter), and the rest of Zion Canyon. See map on p. 36.

3.5 miles RT. Easy. Access: Either the entrance to Watchman Campground, near the amphitheater parking area; or near the Nature Center in South Campground.

Riverside Walk & Gateway to the Narrows ★★   The sound of the rushing Virgin River and the intriguing hanging gardens of wildflowers make this easy paved trail a favorite of ours, as it follows the river upstream to the beginning of the Zion Canyon

Kolob Canyons Area

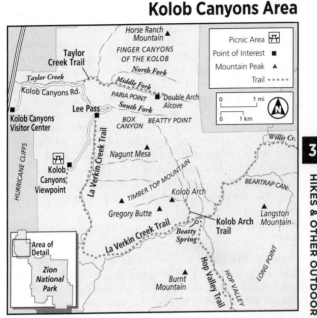

Horse Ranch Mountain ▲

FINGER CANYONS OF THE KOLOB

Taylor Creek Trail

North Fork

Taylor Creek

Kolob Canyons Rd.

Middle Fork

PARIA POINT ■

Double Arch Alcove

Lee Pass

South Fork

■ Kolob Canyons Visitor Center

BOX CANYON

BEATTY POINT

Willis Cr.

Nagunt Mesa

🏕 Kolob Canyons Viewpoint ■

TIMBER TOP MOUNTAIN ▲

Kolob Arch

BEARTRAP CAN.

HURRICANE CLIFFS

Gregory Butte ▲

La Verkin Creek Trail

○ Kolob Arch Trail

Langston Mountain ▲

Beatty Spring

Burnt Mountain ▲

Hop Valley Trail

HOP VALLEY

LONG POINT

Picnic Area 🏕
Point of Interest ■
Mountain Peak ▲
Trail •••••

0 — 1 mi
0 — 1 km

Area of Detail

Zion National Park

3

HIKES & OTHER OUTDOOR PURSUITS IN ZION | Day Hikes

Narrows. It's best in spring and early summer, when the river is at its peak, but the cooling breeze off the river is also refreshing in the summer heat, and the trailside exhibits add interest at any time. Accessible for wheelchair-bound travelers (with some assistance), the trail has an elevation change of only 57 feet over its 2 miles. The pavement ends at the Narrows, and here you can either turn around and head back, or continue upstream into the Narrows, where the canyon walls are sometimes less than 20 feet apart but more than 1,000 feet high. You should have a sturdy hiking staff for wading into the cold river over slippery rocks. Before entering the Narrows, check the weather forecast (posted at Zion Canyon Visitor Center) and discuss your plans with park rangers—during rainstorms (common in July–Aug), flash floods are a serious threat. For more information, see "The Narrows: Safety First" box, on p. 50; the listing on p. 48; and the map on p. 36.

2.2 miles RT. Easy. Access: Temple of Sinawava at the end of Zion Canyon Scenic Dr.

Sand Bench Trail This trail is most popular with hikers in the off-season, as horseback riders use it heavily from March through October. After crossing the river on the footbridge, this sandy trail turns left and meanders through a sagebrush meadow in the Court of the Patriarchs. It's not always well marked, so watch carefully for the junction, where you'll take the left fork across a small stream-bed—after which, the 500-foot climb to the top of the bench begins. Soon the loop splits; if you choose the right fork, you'll pass under sheer stone walls and stark towers until you come out on top, where the Streaked Wall dominates the near view and the Watchman stands sentinel in the distance. As you approach the base of the Streaked Wall, you'll come to a rest area and corral that mark the end of the loop. The trail back takes you along the edge of an escarpment above the river, offering magnificent views of the Twin Brothers, Mountain of the Sun, and East Temple. If you choose the left fork, you'll see all these sights in reverse order, because the trail is a loop. Remember, horses have the right of way, so step to the side of the trail and stand quietly while they pass. See map on p. 36.

3.4-mile loop. Moderate. Access: Court of the Patriarchs Viewpoint, along Zion Canyon Scenic Dr.

Taylor Creek Trail   You will probably get your feet wet as you hike along the Middle Fork of Taylor Creek, fording the water several times. Following the creek bed upstream, you'll have views of Tucupit and Paria points directly ahead, and Horse Ranch Mountain to the left. The Gustav Larson cabin is near the confluence of the North and Middle forks, after which the trail begins its ascent into the canyon between Tucupit and Paria points; it levels out as it follows the creek bed. The Arthur Fife homestead cabin is perched on a bench above the north bank of the creek (p. 30). The trail ends at Double Arch Alcove, a large colorful grotto with an arch high above. The trail has an elevation gain of 450 feet. See map on p. 39.

5 miles RT. Moderate to difficult. Access: Trail head parking area along Kolob Canyons Rd., about 2 miles from Kolob Canyons Visitor Center.

Watchman Trail ★   This moderately strenuous trail gets surprisingly little use, possibly because it can be very hot in the middle of the day. Climbing 368 feet to a plateau near the base of the Watchman formation, it offers splendid views of lower Zion Canyon, Oak Creek Canyon, the Towers of the Virgin, and the West Temple formations. Stay on the main trail, created by the National Park Service—it's 3 feet wide—and avoid the smaller crisscross trails, created by mule deer seeking water and food. The area traversed by the trail is a spring seepage/riparian area rich with a variety of plants—walk quietly and watch for wildlife, especially birds. See map on p. 36.

2.7 miles RT. Moderate. Access: Zion Canyon Visitor Center and Transportation Hub.

> ### Geologic Term: Alcove
>
> An "alcove" is an arch against rock, with no space for light to pass through.

Weeping Rock Trail ★★ ☺ This is among the park's shortest hikes. A self-guided nature trail, with interpretive signs explaining the natural history of the area, takes you through a mixed forest to a rock alcove with lush hanging gardens of ferns and wildflowers. The mist that emanates from the Weeping Rock above is delightfully refreshing on a hot afternoon. Although paved, the trail is relatively steep (gaining 98 ft.) and not suitable for wheelchairs. See map on p. 36.

.4 miles RT. Easy to moderate. Access: Weeping Rock parking lot, on Zion Canyon Scenic Dr.

West Bank of the Virgin River A pleasant hike along the river, this trail affords views of Zion Canyon plus the opportunity to see a myriad of birds, and an occasional mule deer coming out for an early evening drink After crossing the Virgin River at the Court of the Patriarchs Viewpoint, turn left into the middle of the Court to gaze up at the awe-inspiring stone monoliths. Leaving the Court, the trail turns north, levels out, and winds near the river, where you'll be walking amid cottonwood and box elder. As you trek northward, Cathedral Mountain and Mount Majestic slowly rise above you. This section of the trail is used heavily by horseback-riding groups (see "Horseback Riding," later in this chapter).

Once you're past the spur leading east to Zion Lodge across Zion Canyon Scenic Drive, horse traffic comes to an end, and you embark on the wide, paved trail to the Emerald Pools. Follow the main trail up, around, and down to the Lower Pool, bypassing the spur trails leading to the Upper Pools. Follow signs for the Grotto Trail Head as you leave the Lower Pool, winding through lovely rock gardens and past delightful waterfalls. As the trail angles northward again to follow the river, the Great White Throne gradually emerges into view across the river; cross the bridge to the Grotto Trail Head, the end point of your hike.

2.6 miles one-way. Easy. Access: Court of the Patriarchs Viewpoint at the south end, the Grotto Trail Head at the north end, both along Zion Canyon Scenic Dr.

Longer Hikes

Cable Mountain and Deertrap Mountain Trails From the Ponderosa Hunting Club Trail Head, you'll head west into an open ponderosa pine forest, which soon gives way to a meadow of sage-brush, where you join the East Rim Trail (described below). A trail to Echo Canyon heads off to the right; take the left fork for Cable and Deertrap mountains. At the next fork, your route bears right and the East Rim Trail veers left. The trail climbs through juniper, piñon, Gambel oak, and a few ponderosa pines, then tops out in open sagebrush. Here the trail separates: The right branch heads for Cable Mountain, the left for Deertrap Mountain.

The **Cable Mountain Trail** climbs gently to a knoll, from which you can see the more than 10,000-foot-high pink cliffs of the Virgin Rim in the distance, before descending into a manzanita and juniper forest. The trail gradually makes its way northwest along a plateau to the point where pioneers built a cable tramway to carry logs down to the Virgin River. The remains of the tram structure are fragile and very hazardous—please stay back. Look-ing out over the Big Bend of the Virgin River, you have a grand view of the Organ and Angels Landing, with the cliffs of Cathedral Mountain serving as a backdrop. This trail has an elevation gain of 530 feet and a loss of 460 feet.

The **Deertrap Mountain Trail** slopes downward from the junction with Cable Mountain Trail toward the head of Hidden Canyon. As you cross an open area dotted with manzanita, several paths lead to the bottom of a draw (a shallow gully), where there's a small seep (a source of intermittent water that creates the gully). Follow the trail out onto Deertrap Mountain and to the rim of Zion Canyon, for a breathtaking view of the Mountain of the Sun and the Twin Brothers, which are practically in your lap, and the Court of the Patriarchs, which is directly across the canyon. From here, you can walk north and south along the edge of the canyon. The better-defined path runs north (.4 mile) to an overlook, from which you can see the Great White Throne, Angels Landing, and, in the distance, the red tips of the Temple of Sinawava. The southern path (.6 mile) is rough, and leads to a view of the East Temple and Twin Brothers. This trail has an elevation gain of 760 feet and a loss of 470 feet.

These hikes can be combined for an overnight trip from the Ponderosa Hunting Club Trail Head; or for the really zealous, there's the option of combining these hikes with the more strenu-ous East Rim Trail hike (described below), which adds 11.2 miles to the jaunt. See map on p. 36.

6.2 miles RT to Cable Mountain, 7.8 miles RT to Deertrap Mountain, or 11 miles combination RT. Moderate. Access: Ponderosa Hunting Club. From Zion National Park's east entrance drive 2½ miles east on Utah 9, turn north onto the road to the North Fork and Navajo Lake—impassable when wet or snowy—and drive for 5⅓ miles to the Ponderosa Hunting Club. Visitors should register at the small mailbox at the Ponderosa Gate—sign both in and out. Drive through the main entrance and head left [west] on Twin Knolls Rd. for about ¾ mile; turn left south onto Buck Rd. Bear right at the first Y, then left at the next Y, following signs for the Gooder-Reagan cabin. The last few hundred feet descends a rocky grade and crosses a wash, requiring a high-clearance vehicle, before entering the national park at the trail head. Close the gate behind you to keep livestock out.

Chinle Trail ★★ Wonderful distant views, a small petrified forest, a waterfall, and, if your timing is right, an abundance of wildflowers help make this quiet desert trail well worth the 16-mile-plus hike. The first few miles are fairly easy walking along a wide sandy path. Ahead you have views of Mount Kinesava and the Three Marys, and behind are the Eagle Crags. A gradual 150-foot incline brings you to the Petrified Forest. (Please remember, it is illegal to remove anything from the national park; leave the lovely pieces of petrified wood as you find them.) After crossing Huber Wash, the trail heads for Scoggins Wash through more desertlike terrain, with the addition of juniper, piñon, and sagebrush. Once on the mesa beyond Scoggins Wash, the trail moves towards three knolls, passing through several small saddles, traversing a meadow, and crossing the Old Scoggins Stock Trail, built by the area's early pioneers. Continuing west, the trail passes between two knolls and bends around to the north. The final descent into Coalpits Wash brings Cougar Mountain, Smith Mesa, and Lambs Knoll into view; at the bottom you'll find the lovely sight of a pretty waterfall, a bit upstream from Coalpits Spring—the end of the trail. This trail can be uncomfortably hot in summer, but it's an absolute delight November through May, with blankets of wildflowers to dazzle the eye in spring. The elevation gain of this hike is a gradual 550 feet over the first 5 miles. You drop about 250 feet over the last 3 miles. You should plan on a long day for this hike.

16.2 miles RT. Easy to moderate. Access: From the south entrance to the park, drive west on Utah 9 for 3½ miles to a parking area on the right (north) side of the road. From here, follow a marked trail 1.4 miles through a recent real estate development.

East Mesa Trail ★ This is an easier and shorter route to Observation Point than the Observation Point Trail (later in this section), and it is open to equestrians. The trail moves westward over a fairly open plateau through ponderosa pines and manzanita, turning a little to the south as it passes Mystery Canyon; it then winds around a steep unnamed canyon, opening to the south into Echo Canyon, and then passes another canyon to the north that empties into the Virgin River, below the Narrows. Finally the trail connects to Observation Point Trail, just .2 mile from its end; turn right for Observation Point.

6 miles RT. Easy. Access: East Mesa Trail Head. From Zion National Park's east entrance, drive 2½ miles east on Utah 9, turn north onto the road to the North Fork and Navajo Lake—impassable when wet or snowy—and go 5⅓ miles to the Ponderosa Hunting Club. Visitors should register at the small mailbox at the Ponderosa Gate—sign both in and out. Drive through the main entrance and head left (west) on Twin Knolls Rd. for about 1¼ miles to a T intersection; turn right (north) onto Beaver Rd., which deteriorates into little more than a dirt track and eventually reenters the park at the trail head.

East Rim Trail ★   This challenging trail connects with the trails to Cable and Deertrap mountains, Observation Point, and Hidden Canyon (see trail descriptions above), before descending into Zion Canyon at the Weeping Rock Trail Head. Trail intersections are fairly well marked all along the East Rim.

The trail follows an old dirt road up the dry wash of Clear Creek and then begins a climb of about 800 feet up the narrow canyon of Cave Creek. Once on top, you'll follow the rim high above Clear Creek, which affords terrific views of Checkerboard Mesa. At the head of Jolley Gulch, you'll find yourself at a high pour-off, looking down at water-smoothed canyon walls. Leaving the rim, the trail winds along the East Rim Plateau, through scattered piñon and Utah juniper, manzanita, and an occasional Gambel oak in wetter areas. This plateau was heavily logged in the early part of the 20th century (see "Cable Mountain and Deertrap Mountain Trails," above). About 5.3 miles along the trail, you come to a short spur trail over to Stave Spring, an undependable water source (treat before drinking). Soon the trail to Cable and Deertrap mountains branches off to the left, and after another .5 mile the turnoff to the Ponderosa Hunting Club heads right. The East Rim Trail keeps descending toward Echo Canyon, following the top of canyon walls for about .5 mile before following switchbacks down the almost sheer cliffs into Echo Canyon, offering views of Cathedral Mountain and Angels Landing. The trail becomes a mite dicey along here, with twists and turns complicated by slickrock, and rock cairns as the only trail pointers. But finally, you reach the junction with steep Observation Point Trail, which takes off to the right and connects to the East Mesa Trail farther up (see the review of East Mesa Trail above). Don't turn onto Observation Point Trail. Instead, continue down Echo Canyon to the end of the trail at Weeping Rock Trail Head, in Zion Canyon along Zion Canyon Scenic Drive. See map on p. 36.

10.6 miles one-way to Weeping Rock Trail Head. Difficult. Access: Trail head is at the end of a short paved road past a ranger's residence, 450 ft. west of the east entrance to the park.

Observation Point Trail   This hike climbs over 2,000 feet to Observation Point, but the incredible views make all the exertion worthwhile. As you climb the switchbacks that zigzag up the canyon wall, a variety of formations become visible. First there's Angels Landing across the Virgin River, and the Organ a little closer, then the alcove containing Weeping Rock appears to the north. Cathedral Mountain is visible beyond Angels Landing, and the sheer north face of Cable Mountain looms directly overhead. The trail levels out as it enters Echo Canyon. When the East Rim Trail branches off to the right, you head left up the north wall of Echo Canyon, climbing along steep switchbacks, until the trail moves across a steep slope of white cliffs dropping 1,000 feet below the path. When you finally reach the top of the Navajo sandstone formation, the East Mesa Trail heads off to the right, and you bend around to the left through deep sand to Observation Point, right at the tip of the plateau, at an altitude of 6,507 feet. From here you can see far down Zion Canyon; the Great White Throne looms in the foreground with Red Arch Mountain just beyond. For an easier hike to Observation Point, take the East Mesa Trail (see the description above).

8 miles RT. Moderate to difficult. Access: Weeping Rock parking lot along Zion Canyon Scenic Dr.

Wildcat Canyon and Wildcat Canyon Connecting Trails
A high-country trail linking the Hop Valley and West Rim trails (see "Exploring the Backcountry," below), this connector also provides access to several primitive canyon trails. The Wildcat Trail cuts east (right) just a short distance from the Hop Valley Trail Head, passing between Spendlove Knoll to the south and Firepit Knoll to the north, both extinct cinder cones, or simple volcanoes. Crossing the upper end of the Lee Valley takes you through open grassy meadows sprinkled with sagebrush and Gambel oak. Vistas to the east and south include Northgate Peaks, the tops of North and South Guardian Angels above a reddish ridge, the Altar of Sacrifice, the West Temple, and Mount Kinesava. Cedar posts mark the trail, as it becomes obscure in places through the valley. After crossing the Pine Springs Wash, rock cairns point the way along an incline of slickrock.

As you reach the top of the incline, you have a grand unobstructed view of North Guardian Angel. Once past the junctions, with spurs to **Wildcat Canyon Trail Head** and **Northgate Peaks Trail** (the first heads left, the second right—continue straight ahead at both), you begin a gentle incline through a ponderosa pine forest, continuing upward along Russell Gulch. As you enter the headwaters of Wildcat Canyon, you'll see Gambel oak, bigtooth maple, and quaking aspen. The trail descends into the canyon, passing a dependable spring (treat the water before using),

Kolob Plateau Area

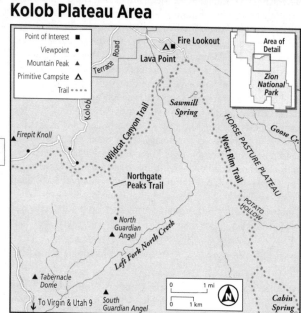

Map legend:
- Point of Interest ■
- Viewpoint •
- Mountain Peak ▲
- Primitive Campsite ▲
- Trail ••••

Fire Lookout
Lava Point
Terrace Road
Kolob
Firepit Knoll
Wildcat Canyon Trail
Sawmill Spring
HORSE PASTURE PLATEAU
Goose Cr.
West Rim Trail
Northgate Peaks Trail
North Guardian Angel
Left Fork North Creek
POTATO HOLLOW
Tabernacle Dome
To Virgin & Utah 9
South Guardian Angel
Cabin Spring

Area of Detail
Zion National Park

0 — 1 mi
0 — 1 km

and then climbs the far wall, eventually reaching the top of the Horse Pasture Plateau. Just before the junction with the West Rim Trail, you'll have fine views of the Lava Point lookout. At the **West Rim Trail,** turn left to reach **Lava Point Trail Head,** the end of the trail. This trail has a total elevation gain of about 1,500 feet, with numerous ups and downs along the way. You should plan on a long day for this hike. See map above.

8.7 miles one-way, Hop Valley Trail Head to Lava Point Trail Head. Moderate. Access: From Virgin, head north on Kolob Terrace Rd. about 13 miles to the parking area for Hop Valley Trail Head.

EXPLORING THE BACKCOUNTRY

There are backpacking opportunities galore here, and several of the day hikes discussed above can be more comfortably done in 2 or more days. In addition to the park's established trails and the famous Narrows, there are a number of off-trail routes for those experienced in the use of compasses and topographic maps—get information at the Zion Canyon Visitor Center. **Backcountry**

permits are required for all overnight hikes in the park as well as for slot canyon hikes. Permits cost $10 for one or two people, $15 for three to seven, and $20 for 8 to 12 people. You can purchase a backcountry permit at the visitor center the day before or the day of your trip, and reservations for permits can be made in advance through the park's website, www.nps.gov/zion, although they must still be picked up in person at the visitor centers. You can get permits at **Zion Canyon Visitor Center,** near the south entrance to the park, or at **Kolob Canyons Visitor Center,** in the northwest corner of the park off I-15. There are also two areas—the Subway and Mystery Canyon—where permits are issued though an online lottery, with a deadline of three months before your planned trip. See the park's Backcountry Planner at www.nps.gov/zion. Backcountry camping is not permitted within 1 mile of a road or trail head.

Hop Valley Trail   This trail loses about 1,050 feet as it meanders northwest through sunny fields and past Gambel oak, partly following an old jeep road and then a stream, before arriving at La Verkin Creek. Many hikers continue on the La Verkin Creek/Kolob Arch trails to see Kolob Arch.

The beginning of the trail takes you through some rather deep sand, so if your gear includes gaiters (cloth or leather leg coverings that keep the sand out), wear them. After passing through the hiker gate in the fence, marking the beginning of an inholding (privately owned property within the park), you'll be sharing space with cattle from spring through fall. Follow the four-wheel-drive road, marked by fence posts when it becomes almost too faint to see, until you reach the stream at the bottom of Hop Valley. Follow the stream or cattle trails along it down the valley, and shortly Langston Canyon will come in from the right, sometimes contributing a trickle of water to the stream. About .5 mile farther, another fence marks the end of the inholding, and the stream sinks into the sand and disappears in summer. A sign marks where the trail leaves the wash and climbs a hill. After climbing the hill, the trail follows a steep descent into the valley of La Verkin Creek. Camping is allowed outside the inholding, and shady sites can be found among the pines not far from the wash. From here you can head to Kolob Arch, about .75 miles away, explore the La Verkin Creek system, or return to the Hop Valley Trail Head. If you see any cattle outside the inholding, notify the Park Service when you finish your hike. Hikers should plan on allotting a full day for this walk. See map on p. 39.

13.4 miles RT. Moderate to difficult. Access: Trail head on Kolob Terrace Rd., about 13 miles north of Virgin.

La Verkin Creek/Kolob Arch Trails ★ La Verkin Creek and its tributaries are responsible for the magnificent canyons cut into the red Navajo sandstone in this section of the park. This hike passes through dry sagebrush flats and forests of conifers, cottonwoods, and box elders; and where water seeps from the stone, hanging gardens astonish the eye. This trail is popular and can be quite busy on summer weekends, in spite of the almost 800-foot net elevation gain of the return trek. From the trail head, you descend to Timber Creek, which is often dry by late summer. Follow it upstream around the base of Shuntavi Butte, Timber Top Mountain, and Gregory Butte; as you climb into a small open bowl, the views widen to the south and east. Soon you'll come to an old corral built by Mormon pioneers, after which there is a short side hike downstream to a series of pretty, though short, waterfalls. Follow La Verkin Creek upstream along the north bank, with Gregory Butte towering overhead on your left and Neagle Ridge jutting up on the right.

When you reach the turnoff to the Kolob Arch Viewpoint, turn left along a tiny tributary with some steep ups and downs on rocky footing for about .5 mile. Then look up—Kolob Arch soars high overhead about .25 mile away. One of the largest arches in the world, it measures over 300 feet wide. **Caution:** Going beyond the viewpoint is not recommended, due to the instability of the slopes. Back on the main trail a short way upstream, cross over to Beatty Spring, the official end of this trail, after which you'll find the junction with **Hop Valley Trail** (heading southeast). You've come about 7 miles and descended to 5,200 feet of elevation. Further exploration upstream takes you to Beartrap Canyon and then up Willis Creek, another 4.5 miles with a further elevation loss of just under 200 feet.

Some people choose to camp on this hike. You can camp at La Verkin Creek, if you have a permit and have been assigned a campsite at the visitor center. See map on p. 39.

14 miles RT. Moderate heading east, strenuous returning west. Access: Kolob Canyons Rd., at Lee Pass.

The Narrows ★★★ Exploring the Narrows involves wading along the bottom of the North Fork of the Virgin River, through a spectacular 1,000-foot-deep chasm that is less than 20 feet wide in spots. Passing fancifully sculptured sandstone arches, hanging gardens, and waterfalls, this hike is recommended for those who are up to fighting sometimes-strong currents. If you want just a taste of the Narrows, walk and wade in from the other end, from the **Riverside Walk** (listed earlier in this chapter).

The full trip through the Narrows involves a long day or preferably a 2-day trek, and entails arranging a ride to the trail head and then catching a park shuttle at the Temple of Sinawava, where you leave the canyon at the end of your journey. From the trail head, on private land, you'll ford the river and follow a dirt road downstream. (Please remain on the road and leave all gates as found.) The road ends a short distance beyond an old cabin, and from here you will hike either along or in the river, which cuts a deep canyon into the Navajo sandstone. The walls are broken only by an occasional steeply ridged canyon, created over millennia by some seemingly insignificant stream in its quest to reach the Virgin River. You'll come up against a 12-foot waterfall—a path circumnavigates this natural barrier by leading you through a slot in the rock.

You are now within the boundary of the park, and in another 1.5 miles, you will reach the confluence with Deep Creek, where the canyon widens to absorb this sizable flow of water. In the next 2 miles lie the designated—and assigned—campsites. The current here is faster, due to the increased flow of water, and the rocks underfoot are slippery, so step carefully to avoid injury. Kolob Creek is the next tributary seen, though it flows only when waters are released from Kolob Reservoir for irrigation downstream; Goose Creek comes in next and signals a deepening of the water—waist-high in some places—and an increase in the speed of the flow. Soon you'll see Big Springs gushing over moss-covered stone on the right wall of the canyon, signifying the beginning of the Narrows.

For the next 3 miles, there is no place to climb out of the water in the event of a flash flood, and there is practically no vegetation to grab onto, as any small seedling is periodically ripped from its hold by raging waters. (See the box "The Narrows: Safety First," below.) The river spreads from wall to wall, requiring constant wading in a deep canyon with little light. The water has even undercut the walls near the confluence with Orderville Canyon. Runoff from above oozes from the canyon walls here, providing moisture for hanging gardens and habitat for the minuscule Zion snail, found nowhere else in the world (see chapter 9, "A Nature Guide to Zion & Bryce Canyon National Parks"). About a mile farther, where the canyon opens out, a narrow ribbon of water slips out of Mystery Canyon above, and skims down the rounded canyon wall. Just beyond, you can finally climb out of the water onto the paved **Riverside Walk** that takes you to the Temple of Sinawava and the end of the hike.

Permits are required for full-day and overnight hikes originating from Chamberlain's Ranch. Walk-in permits are available the day

THE NARROWS: safety first

Hiking in the **Narrows,** which are subject to flash flooding, can be treacherous, as there are many sections where there is no place to escape a rushing wall of water. Hiking here is not advised when rain is forecast or threatening; park officials strongly recommend that hikers check the latest National Weather Service forecast before setting out, even when skies appear clear. Weather forecasts are posted at the Zion Canyon Visitor Center, and rangers are available to discuss current conditions, but park officials emphasize that all hikers are responsible for their own safety.

Even those planning just a short day hike into the Narrows, entering from the end of the Riverside Walk, need to spend some time on preparation. Hikers should wear sturdy boots or shoes with good ankle support that they won't mind getting wet; carry an empty bag to pack out all trash; take drinking water, sunscreen, and a first-aid kit; be prepared for cold temperatures with a sweater or jacket; and put everything in waterproof containers. Equipment can be rented from **Zion Adventure Company** (p. 34).

Experienced Narrows hikers also recommend that you take a walking stick to help steady yourself against the strong currents. Sticks are sometimes available near the end of the Riverside Walk, but you're better off taking your own. Hikers are prohibited from cutting tree branches to make walking sticks. Because there are no restrooms in the Narrows, hikers should use the restroom at the Riverside Walk Trail Head before heading out. Park officials request that human waste be buried as far away from the river and other water sources as possible.

Because of strong currents and deep pools, park officials recommend kids under 4'8" tall not hike in the river.

before or the day of your trip at the Zion Canyon Visitor Center; campsites are assigned and the number of hikers, both day and overnight, is limited. Backcountry reservations are also available online via the park's website, www.nps.gov/zion, although the permits must still be picked up in person at the visitor center. Short day hikes, starting and ending at the end of the Riverside Walk, do not require permits.

Several local companies, including **Zion Adventure Company** (p. 34), offer guided trips through the Narrows, with rates starting at $149 per person for two or more people.

16 miles one-way. Difficult. Permit required. Access: Chamberlain's Ranch (outside the park); arrange a shuttle for delivery and pickup; see the introduction to this chapter for shuttle information. From Zion National Park's east entrance, drive 2½ miles east on Utah 9, turn north onto the road to the North Fork and Navajo Lake—impassable when wet or snowy—and go 18 miles. Immediately after crossing the bridge over the Virgin River, turn left onto a gravel road, and go 1 mile to the trail head, which is just before the river ford.

West Rim Trail ★ This trail has a net elevation loss of 3,400 feet over 14.5 miles to the Grotto Picnic Area, and many hikers choose to arrange for a shuttle rather than attempting the strenuous climb back to Lava Point—most of the rise is achieved in the first 6 miles from the south end. The easiest way to do this is to leave your car at the south end (lowest point) and get a shuttle to the top to begin your hike.

Over half of this very popular hike is spent atop the Horse Pasture Plateau, a finger of land pointing toward Angels Landing, which affords incredible vistas all along the trail. The plateau boasts a wide range of plant life, and consequently, a fascinating variety of birds and animals. The many blackened trees attest to the numerous lightning strikes that have occurred here. You'll also find stark reminders of a 1980 wildfire.

At the southern end of the plateau, you can choose to take the **Telephone Canyon Trail** or stay on the Rim Route; the first is a little shorter, and they come together again at West Rim Spring Junction, just before the steep descent into Zion Canyon. The climb down takes you around and behind Mount Majestic and Cathedral Mountain, following part of Refrigerator Canyon, and connects to **Angels Landing Trail** before depositing you at the Grotto Picnic Area. See map on p. 46.

29 miles RT. Difficult. Access: Lava Point Trail Head. From Virgin, take Kolob Terrace Rd. north about 21 miles, turn right toward Lava Point; after about a mile, there's a fork: If it's dry, take the left fork and drive about 1⅓ miles to the trail head; otherwise, take the right fork to Lava Point Campground, where there's a connecting trail to the trail head.

BIKING & MOUNTAIN BIKING

Although bikes are forbidden on almost all trails, and cross-country biking is prohibited within the national park boundaries, Zion is among the West's most bike-friendly national parks. The bike-friendly **Pa'rus Trail** runs a little under 2 miles along the Virgin River, from the south park entrance and South Campground to Zion Canyon Scenic Drive, crossing the river and several creeks, and providing good views of the Watchman, West Temple, the Sentinel, and other lower-canyon formations. The trail is paved

Bikers Beware

If you have a bike rack on the rear bumper of your car, keep the bike tires far from the exhaust pipe; one bike shop worker told us he did a good business replacing exhaust-cooked bike tires.

and open to bicyclists, pedestrians, pets on leashes, and those with strollers or wheelchairs, but is closed to cars. See the last paragraph of this section for information on where to rent bikes.

From April through October, the **Zion Canyon Scenic Drive,** beyond its intersection with the Zion–Mt. Carmel Highway, is closed to private motor vehicles, with the exception of motorists who have reservations at Zion Lodge. However, the road is open to hikers and bicyclists, as well as shuttle buses. Bicyclists should pull to the right road shoulder and stop to allow shuttle buses to pass.

Bicycles can also be ridden on other park roads, but not through the Zion–Mt. Carmel Tunnel.

Although mountain bikes are prohibited on the trails of Zion National Park (except the Pa'rus Trail), just outside the park—mostly on Bureau of Land Management and state-owned property—are numerous rugged jeep trails that are great for mountain biking, plus more than 100 miles of slickrock cross-country trails and single-track trails. **Gooseberry Mesa,** above the community of Springdale, is generally considered the best mountain-biking destination in the area, but there are also good trails on nearby **Grafton Mesa.**

Talk with the knowledgeable staff at **Zion Cycles** (p. 34) about the best trails for your interests and abilities. This full-service bike shop offers a full range of bikes, maps, accessories, repairs, and rentals ($38–$55 for a full day, $28–$45 for a half-day).

For guided mountain or road bike trips, contact **Zion Adventure Company** (p. 34). A guided hike and road bike trip into the park costs $139 for a half-day and $179 for a full day, per person for two people, with lower per-person rates for larger groups. **Zion Rock & Mountain Guides** (p. 34) also offers guided mountain bike excursions outside the national park at similar rates.

OTHER SPORTS & ACTIVITIES

FISHING   Though not the most popular pastime in the park, fishing in the Virgin River is permitted with a valid Utah fishing license, available at sporting goods stores and other businesses throughout Utah; contact the **Utah Division of Wildlife**

Resources, 1594 W. North Temple, Ste. 2110 (P.O. Box 146301), Salt Lake City, UT 84114-6301 (✆ **801/538-4700;** www.wild life.utah.gov), for more details. Anglers occasionally catch a few trout, but the stream is not stocked.

HORSEBACK RIDING   Horseback riding is permitted in many areas of the park—it's especially popular in the Kolob Canyons section—although it is prohibited on some of the more popular hiking trails. Backcountry permits (p. 46) are required for overnight trips into the backcountry. For complete details on overnight horseback riding trips, contact the park offices (see chapter 10, "Planning Your Trip to Zion & Bryce Canyon National Parks") and ask for a copy of the free handout "Pack Animal Use." People bring their own horses for the trips.

Guided rides in the park are available March through October from **Canyon Trail Rides,** P.O. Box 128, Tropic, UT 84776 (✆ **435/679-8665;** www.canyonrides.com), with ticket sales and information near Zion Lodge. A 1-hour ride along the Virgin River costs $40, and a half-day ride on the Sand Beach Trail costs $75. Riders must weigh no more than 220 pounds, and children must be at least 7 years old for the 1-hour ride and 10 years old for the half-day ride. Reservations are advised.

ROCK CLIMBING   Expert technical rock climbers like the tall sandstone cliffs in Zion Canyon, although rangers warn that much of the rock is loose, or "rotten," and climbing equipment and techniques that are suitable for granite are often less effective (and therefore less safe) on sandstone. Backcountry permits, available at visitor centers, are required for overnight climbs and cost $10 for one or two persons, $15 for three to seven, and $20 for 8 to 12 people. Because some routes may be closed at times, such as during peregrine falcon nesting, from early spring through July, climbers should check at the Zion Canyon Visitor Center before setting out. **Zion Adventure Company** and **Zion Rock & Mountain Guides** (p. 34) offer a variety of guided rock climbing and hiking trips, as well as instruction. Typical per-person rates are $125 for a half-day and $160 for a full day for two people, with lower per-person rates for larger groups. Zion Rock & Mountain Guides also offers equipment rentals and sales.

Climbers without the necessary expertise for Zion are advised to try nearby Snow Canyon State Park (see chapter 8, "Nearby Things to See & Do").

SWIMMING & TUBING   Hikers in the Narrows soon find that they are participating in a water sport, as they wade along the "trail" at the bottom of the Virgin River. Swimming and wading are prohibited in the Emerald Pools. Swimming is permitted in the Virgin River south of South Campground amphitheater; check with the visitor center about other areas that would be safe for swimming. Those wanting to go tubing in the river can rent tubes ($15) from **Zion Adventure Company** (p. 34).

WINTER ACTIVITIES   Zion does not usually get enough snow for winter sports, but the relatively warm winter days can be perfect for hiking. However, winter hikers need to be especially careful when trails are icy.

Other Sports & Activities

HIKES & OTHER OUTDOOR PURSUITS IN ZION

WHERE TO STAY, CAMP & EAT IN ZION

L odging, eating, and camping choices inside the park are limited to Zion Lodge and the three National Park Service campgrounds, which are wonderful and allow you to spend the most time possible in the park, enjoying changing angles of the sun's rays on the rocks. In addition to using the park's lodging, dining, and camping options, you'll probably head to the nearby gateway communities for at least some of your eating and lodging, and possibly camping. Generally, the farther you get from the park entrances, the less expensive your lodging will be. Outside the park, you'll find choices to suit almost every taste.

WHERE TO STAY

Pets are not accepted unless otherwise noted. Room tax adds 10.2% in the park and 12.8% outside the park. For additional information about lodging, dining, and other services in the area contact the **Zion Canyon Visitors Bureau,** P.O. Box 331, Springdale, UT 84767 (*©* **888/ 518-7070;** www.zionpark.com).

Inside the Park

Zion Lodge ★★★ This handsome lodge is a wonderful place to stay, but the main draw is its location. Built in 1925 by the Union Pacific Railroad, the lodge was destroyed by fire in 1966, then rebuilt and restored to its historic appearance. The only lodging inside the park, Zion Lodge sits in a valley with spectacular views of the park's rock cliffs. The charming and genuinely historic cabins are our first choice here because they perfectly fit the national park ambience. Each has a private porch, stone (gas-burning) fireplace, two queen-size or double beds, and pine walls. The comfortable modern motel units are just that, with two queen-size beds and a private porch or balcony. The plush motel suites are spacious, with one king-size bed, a separate sitting room with a queen-size hide-a-bed, and a refrigerator. Ranger programs are presented in the lodge auditorium in summer. All units are nonsmoking.

Zion National Park, UT. www.zionlodge.com. ⓒ **435/772-7700.** Information and reservations: Xanterra Parks & Resorts, Central Reservations, 6312 S. Fiddlers Green Circle, Ste. 600N, Greenwood Village, CO 80111. ⓒ **888/297-2757** or 303/297-2757. Fax 303/297-3175. 121 units. Mid-Mar to Nov motel rooms $170 double; cabins $180 double; suites $186 double. Discounts (sometimes up to 50% off) and packages available at other times. AE, DISC, MC, V. **Amenities:** 2 restaurants (Red Rock Grill and Castle Dome cafe; see reviews, p. 64). *In room:* A/C.

Outside the Park

See chapter 8, "Nearby Things to See & Do," for a discussion of things to see and do in these gateway communities.

SPRINGDALE

Best Western Zion Park Inn ★   This is a good choice for those who are seeking an upscale, reliable chain motel, with possibly even a few pleasant surprises. Rooms in the handsome two-story complex, located 1½ miles from the park, are tastefully appointed in Southwest style, with either two queen beds or one king-size bed, light-colored walls decorated with artwork depicting the area, and solid wood furnishings. Especially appealing are the units with pitched, high ceilings, with windows that seem to be aligned precisely to capture the views of the colorful rock formations outside. The grounds are nicely landscaped, and of course offer phenomenal views of the area's red rock formations.

1215 Zion Park Blvd., Springdale, UT 84767. www.zionparkinn.com. ⓒ **800/934-7275** or 435/772-3200. Fax 435/772-2449. 120 units. Mar–Oct $115–$135 double; $140–$180 suite or family unit; Nov–Feb $68–$85 double, $90–$130 suite or family unit. No charge for children 17 and under. AE, DC, DISC, MC, V. 1 pet accepted, for an extra fee of $25. **Amenities:** Restaurant; sports bar; heated outdoor pool (Mar–Oct only); putting green; hot tub; volleyball and badminton courts; basketball hoop; liquor store. *In room:* A/C, TV, hair dryer.

Canyon Ranch Motel   Consisting of a series of two- and four-unit cottages set back from the highway, this motel's buildings simply ooze charm, with the look of 1930s-style cabins on the outside while providing modern motel rooms inside. Rooms are either new or newly remodeled, and options include one queen- or king-size bed, two queen-size beds, or one queen-size and one double. Some rooms have showers only, while others have tub/shower combos. Room no. 13, with two queen-size beds, offers

Gateways to Zion & Bryce Canyon

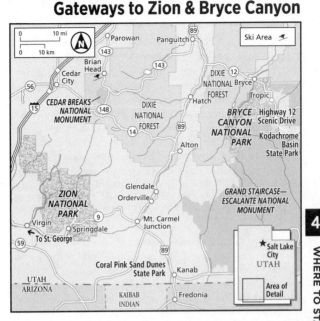

spectacular views of the Zion National Park rock formations; views from most other rooms are almost as good. The units surround a lawn with trees and picnic tables. All units are nonsmoking.

668 Zion Park Blvd. (P.O. Box 175), Springdale, UT 84767. www.canyonranch motel.com. (℡) **866/946-6276** or 435/772-3357. 22 units. Apr-Oct $99-$119 double, kitchenettes $139; Nov-Mar $69-$89 double; kitchenettes $109. AE, DISC, MC, V. Pets accepted in some units, only one or two dogs per unit ($24 fee first night, $12 second night, $6 third night). **Amenities:** Outdoor pool (Apr-Oct only); hot tub. *In room:* A/C, TV, kitchenettes (some units), Wi-Fi.

Cliffrose Lodge & Gardens ★ With delightful river frontage and 5 acres of lawns, shade trees, and flower gardens, the Cliffrose offers a beautiful setting just outside the entrance to Zion National Park. The architecture is Southwestern adobe style, with redwood balconies, and the outdoor rock waterfall whirlpool tub is a delight, especially in the evening. Modern, well-kept rooms have all the standard motel appointments, with unusually large bathrooms with tub/shower combinations. We especially like the four very luxurious Canyon View Suites, which sleep up to six guests each. On the lawns, you'll find comfortable seating, including a lawn swing. All units are nonsmoking.

281 Zion Park Blvd., Springdale, UT 84767. www.cliffroselodge.com. ℂ **800/243-8824** or 435/772-3234. 50 units. Apr–Oct and holidays $149–$199 per unit; rates lower at other times. AE, DISC, MC, V. **Amenities:** Large outdoor heated pool (Apr–Oct only); whirlpool; playground. *In room:* A/C, TV, fridge, Wi-Fi.

Desert Pearl Inn ★ This riverside property offers luxurious and comfortable rooms and suites with beautiful views of the area's scenery from private terraces or balconies. Spacious rooms are decorated in modern Southwest style, with either two queen beds or one king-size bed, and each room also has a queen-size sofa sleeper. Bathrooms are two rooms: One with a tub/shower combo, toilet, and bidet; the other with a closet, vanity, and sink. The grounds are nicely landscaped. All units are nonsmoking.

707 Zion Park Blvd., Springdale, UT 84767. www.desertpearl.com. ℂ **888/828-0898** or 435/772-8888. Fax 435/772-8889. 61 units. Summer $158–$188 double, $298 suite; winter $98–$118 double, $198 suite. AE, DISC, MC, V. **Amenities:** Huge outdoor heated pool (Apr–Oct only); whirlpool. *In room:* A/C, TV, fridge, hair dryer, microwave, minibar, Wi-Fi.

Driftwood Lodge Beautiful lawns and gardens enhance this attractive, well-kept motel—a quiet, lush complex perfect for sitting back and admiring the spectacular rock formations that practically surround the town. The spacious rooms have light walls and wood-grain furnishings; all have patios or balconies. Most standard rooms have two queen-size beds; others have one king-size. Two family suites each have one king-size and two queen-size beds, and the handsome king suites have a separate sitting room, king-size bed, and a microwave. The restaurant has a delightful outdoor patio with splendid views into the national park.

1515 Zion Park Blvd. (P.O. Box 447), Springdale, UT 84767. www.driftwoodlodge. net. ℂ **888/801-8811** or 435/772-3262. Fax 435/772-3702. 53 units. Apr–Nov $129–$149 double, $169–$209 family unit and suite; Dec–Mar $59–$79 double, $89–$129 family unit and suite. AE, DC, DISC, MC, V. Pets accepted at management's discretion, $25 fee. **Amenities:** Restaurant; outdoor heated pool (Apr–Oct only); whirlpool; Wi-Fi. *In room:* A/C, TV, fridge, microwave, hair dryer.

Flanigan's Inn ★★★ A mountain-lodge atmosphere suffuses this very attractive complex of natural wood and rock set among trees, lawns, and flowers, just outside the entrance to Zion National Park. This is a place where you will actually want to spend time relaxing. The rooms are artfully decorated in a spa-like atmosphere, with top-line amenities. Most units have decks or patios and large windows overlooking a natural courtyard, including a koi pond, heated pool, and hot tub. Suites have microwaves in addition to small refrigerators, and the two completely furnished villas are beautifully decorated upscale homes separate from the main inn. A nature trail leads to a hilltop labyrinth and spectacular vistas. There is a full-service spa, including a salon and yoga exercise room, and bicycles are available for guests' use. The inn is 50% wind powered and entirely nonsmoking.

450 Zion Park Blvd., Springdale, UT 84767. www.flanigans.com. (🕾) **800/765-7787** or 435/772-3244. Fax 435/772-3396. 36 units. Mid-Mar through Nov and holidays $129–$169 double, $249–$359 suites and villas; lower rates at other times. AE, DISC, MC, V. **Amenities:** Restaurant (Spotted Dog Café; see review, p. 65); outdoor heated pool (Apr–Oct only); outdoor hot tub; full-service spa. *In room:* A/C, TV, fridge, hair dryer, Wi-Fi.

Harvest House Bed & Breakfast at Zion ★★

Personal touches and yummy breakfasts make this B&B a fine alternative to a standard motel. Built in 1989, the house is Utah territorial-style (similar to Victorian), with a garden sitting area with a koi pond and spectacular views of the national park's rock formations. Rooms are charming, comfortable, and quiet, with king- or queen-size beds and private bathrooms. The units are furnished with an eclectic mix of contemporary items, and original art peppers the walls. One upstairs room faces west and has grand sunset views, while the other two have private decks facing the impressive formations of Zion.

There's a big-screen TV in the living room with access to some 40 movie channels; and the gourmet breakfasts are sumptuous, with fresh-baked breads, fresh-squeezed orange juice, granola, fruit, yogurt, and a hot main course. All units are nonsmoking.

29 Canyon View Dr., Springdale, UT 84767. www.harvesthouse.net. (🕾) **800/719-7493** or 435/772-3880. 4 units. $100–$135 double. Rates include full breakfast. DISC, MC, V. Children 7 and older welcome. **Amenities:** Outdoor hot tub. *In room:* A/C, Wi-Fi, no phone.

Historic Pioneer Lodge and Restaurant ★

Old West ambience and style with modern amenities and comfortable beds are what you'll find at the Historic Pioneer Lodge. Standard rooms have a homey feel with one king- or two queen-size beds and some of the quietest heating/air conditioning units around (and heating and cooling is all remote control). There are 40 rooms and three suites, and all units have rustic log furnishings, good lighting, full carpeting, and granite counters. On the premises is a gift shop selling the work of Southern Utah artists, an Internet cafe, and a reasonably priced restaurant where lodge guests receive a 10% discount during their stay. All units are nonsmoking.

838 Zion Park Blvd., Springdale, UT 84767. www.pioneerlodge.com. (🕾) **888/772-3233** or 435/772-3233. 43 units. Summer $164–$186 double; $208–$329 suite; lower rates the rest of the year. AE, DISC, MC, V. **Amenities:** Restaurant; outdoor heated pool (Apr–Oct only); whirlpool. *In room:* A/C, TV, fridge, hair dryer, microwave, Wi-Fi.

Majestic View Lodge ★★   Virtually every room at this complex of two-storey stucco and log buildings offers a stunning view of the surrounding rock formations. The cozy, spotless rooms all have patios or balconies, and are furnished with rustic aspen decor (the deluxe suites have kitchenettes). Spend some time at the restaurant or saloon—both sharing the excellent views—or visit the Lodge's sprawling trading post and wildlife museum. A free shuttle to the park leaves regularly from the lodge's property.

2400 Zion Park Blvd, Springdale, UT 84767. www.majesticviewlodge.com. ℰ **866/772-0665** or 435/772-0665. 69 units. Apr–Oct $159–$169 double; Nov–Mar $89 double. AE, DC, DISC, MC, V. **Amenities:** Restaurant; bar; brew pub; heated outdoor pool; hot tub; laundry; store; wildlife museum. *In room:* A/C, TV, fridge, Wi-Fi.

Under the Eaves Inn ★★   This romantic 1931 home, located in the heart of Springdale, offers handsomely decorated historic rooms, beautiful gardens and shade trees, and spectacular views from what innkeepers Joe Pitti and Mark Chambers call "the best front porch in Utah." The units range from the basic Hiker's Room to a luxurious suite—covering 1,200-square feet, it has a vaulted ceiling, a wood-burning stove, a kitchenette, and a claw-foot tub plus separate shower. The cute Garden Cottage, built in 1928 was moved here from inside the national park. It contains two small but comfortable rooms on the main floor and the more rustic lower level hikers' room. Breakfast is off the menu at nearby Oscar's Cafe, served from 7 to 11am. All units are nonsmoking.

980 Zion Park Blvd. (P.O. Box 29), Springdale, UT 84767. www.undertheeaves. com. ℰ **866/261-2655** or 435/772-3457. 6 units. $85–$150 double, $185 suite. Rates include full breakfast. AE, DISC, MC, V. Children allowed at management's discretion. *In room:* A/C, Wi-Fi, no phone.

Zion Park Motel   This economical motel is another good choice for travelers on a budget, offering comfortable, attractively furnished rooms with showers or tub/shower combos. Standard rooms are a bit small, especially with the refrigerator and microwave they all have, but the light-colored wood furnishings and walls help make them feel bigger. The one king- or two queen-size beds have colorful spreads, and art depicting the region decorates the walls. The family units sleep six. All units are nonsmoking.

865 Zion Park Blvd. (P.O. Box 365), Springdale, UT 84767. www.zionparkmotel. com. 21 units. $84 double; $104–$149 family unit and suite. AE, DISC, MC, V. **Amenities:** Outdoor heated pool (Apr–Oct only); picnic area; playground. *In room:* A/C, TV, fridge, microwave, full kitchens (in 2 units), Wi-Fi.

NEAR THE EAST ENTRANCE TO ZION NATIONAL PARK

Although there is no town directly outside the east entrance to Zion National Park, several businesses provide visitor services nearby. About 13 miles east of the east entrance, at the junction of Utah 9 and U.S. 89, is Mt. Carmel Junction, at an elevation of 5,191 feet. The town is 73 miles southwest of Bryce Canyon National Park, and 17 miles northwest of Kanab.

For area information, contact the **Kane County Office of Tourism,** 78 S. 100 E., Kanab, UT 84741 (© **800/733-5263** or 435/644-5033; www.kaneutah.com).

Best Western East Zion Thunderbird Lodge ★ A well-maintained two-story motel with Southwest decor, the Thunderbird offers quiet, spacious, comfortable rooms, with king- or queen-size beds, wood furnishings, photos or artwork depicting area scenery, and a private balcony or patio. The lodging has a gas station and a convenience store on the premises. All rooms are nonsmoking. Also under the same management, with the same contact information, is a nearby house with two bedrooms, each with their own bathroom, a living room with a fireplace and vaulted ceiling, and a large fully-equipped kitchen for $295 for up to six people (minimum 2-day rental). The complex also includes a campground, the East Zion Riverside RV Park. (See "Camping," below.)

At the junction of Utah 9 and U.S. 89 (P.O. Box 5536), Mt. Carmel Junction, UT 84755. www.zionnational-park.com. © **888/848-6358** or 435/648-2203. Fax 435/648-2239. 61 units. May–Oct $114–$129 double; Nov–Mar $73–$83. AE, DC, DISC, MC, V. **Amenities:** Restaurant (Thunderbird Restaurant; see review, p. 66); large outdoor heated pool (Apr–Oct only); 9-hole golf course; whirlpool. *In room:* A/C, TV, fridge (in some), hair dryer, microwave (in some), Wi-Fi.

Zion Mountain Ranch ★ The upscale log cabins and family lodges here, just outside the east entrance to the national park, provide a luxurious way to "rough it" while visiting Zion. The spacious log cabins have lodgepole king-size beds and plenty of amenities. The basic cabins range from 325 to 450 square feet and have one or two king-size beds and gas fireplaces. There are also larger and more upscale cabin suites and what are called family lodges—1,000 to 1,500 square feet—that sleep from 7 to 10 people and include fully equipped kitchens. The property covers 1,000 partly wooded acres, where you're very likely to see the resort's bison herd. There is hiking, horseback riding ($35 for a 1-hour ride), and fishing ponds. All units are nonsmoking.

9065 W. Utah 9, Mt. Carmel, UT 84755 (3 miles east of the Zion National Park east entrance). www.zionmountainresort.com. © **866/648-2555** or 435/648-2555. 50 units. Apr–Oct $145–$166 double in cabin, $166–$295 cabin suite, $309–$471 family lodge; Nov–Mar $99–$119 double in cabin, $135–$206 cabin suite, $229–$379 family lodge. AE, DISC, MC, V. **Amenities:** Restaurant; outdoor whirlpool tub. *In room:* A/C, TV/DVD player, fridge, microwave, no phone.

CAMPING

Pets are accepted at all campgrounds listed here, but they must be leashed (see pet restrictions at Zion Canyon Campground, below).

Inside the Park

The two developed **national park campgrounds** in Zion Canyon are the best places to camp while visiting the park, if you can find a site. Both of the park's main campgrounds—**South** ★★ and **Watchman** ★★★—are located just inside the park's south entrance. They have paved roads, well-spaced sites, some trees, and that national park atmosphere that you came here to enjoy. There are restrooms with flush toilets, and sites for those with disabilities. Although there are no RV hookups at South Campground, electric hookups are available in two loops in Watchman. **Lava Point,** a free primitive campground about an hour's drive from Zion Canyon, is located on the Kolob Terrace. It has fire grates, tables, and vault toilets, but no water. The access road to Lava Point is restricted to vehicles 19 feet long or less.

Reservations for Watchman Campground can be made from early March through November (© **877/444-6777;** www.recreation. gov). Of Watchman Campground's 164 sites, 95 have electric hookups and 69 are available only to those camping in tents.

Some campers without reservations stay at nearby commercial campgrounds their first night in the area, and then hurry to the

Amenities for Each Campground, Zion National Park

CAMPGROUND	ELEV.	TOTAL SITES	RV HOOK-UPS	DUMP STATION	TOILETS	DRINKING WATER
Lava Point	7,890	6	0	no	yes	no
South	4,000	127	0	yes	yes	yes
Watchman	4,000	164	95	yes	yes	yes
East Zion Riverside	5,191	12	12	yes	yes	yes
Zion Canyon	3,800	200	125	yes	yes	yes

park campgrounds the next morning, circling like vultures until a site becomes available.

There are no showers in the national park, but the commercial campgrounds listed below offer showers, for a fee, to those camping in the park.

Outside the Park

Just outside the east and south park entrances are commercial campgrounds with hot showers and RV hookups. Keep in mind that the park's visitor center, campgrounds, and most of its developed attractions are closer to the south entrance than to the east.

East Zion Riverside RV Park is located in the Best Western East Zion Thunderbird Lodge complex in Mt. Carmel Junction, about 13 miles east of the east entrance to the national park (P.O. Box 5536, Mt. Carmel Junction, UT 84755; ✆ **435/648-2203;** www.zionnational-park.com). Especially good for self-contained RVs, the park sits along the banks of the East Fork of the Virgin River in the shade of cottonwood trees, and offers campers use of the pool, hot tub, and other amenities at the adjacent Thunderbird Lodge. All sites are back-in.

Zion Canyon Campground ★ is at 479 Zion Park Blvd., Springdale, UT 84767, a half-mile south of the park's south entrance (✆ **435/772-3237;** www.zioncamp.com). Although quite crowded in summer, the campground is clean and well maintained, with tree-shaded sites and grassy tent areas. There are also especially large sites for big RVs. Some sites are along the Virgin River, and the campground has free cable TV hookups, a swimming pool, a game room, a playground, and a store. Dogs are permitted at RV sites but not tent sites. There is a Quality Inn (42 units) on the grounds (✆ **435/772-3237;** fax 435/772-3844), with rates of $120 to $150 for a double year-round.

SHOWERS	FIRE PITS/ GRILLS	LAUNDRY	RESERVE	FEES	OPEN
no	yes	no	no	Free	June through Oct
no	yes	no	no	$16	Early Mar through Oct
no	yes	no	yes	$16–$20	Year-round
no	no	yes	yes	$15	Year-round
yes	yes	yes	yes	$30–$35	Year-round

In addition to the two commercial campgrounds discussed here, there is also camping at Cedar Breaks National Monument and Snow Canyon State Park. (See chapter 8, "Nearby Things to See & Do.")

WHERE TO EAT

Those looking for picnic supplies won't find any stores inside Zion National Park, but Springdale, just outside the park's south entrance, has several stores. See the Fast Facts entry for "Supplies," in chapter 10, "Fast Facts."

Inside the Park

Castle Dome Cafe ☺ SNACK BAR   At the north end of the lodge, this simple fast food restaurant offers an outdoor dining patio serving cinnamon buns, burgers, sandwiches, hot dogs, pizza, ice cream, frozen yogurt, and similar fare. No alcoholic beverages are served.

Zion National Park. ℂ **435/772-3213.** Menu items $4–$10. No credit cards. Summer daily 7am–9pm; shorter hours the rest of the year.

Red Rock Grill ★★ AMERICAN   Try to have at least one meal here during your national park vacation. The restaurant's mountain lodge decor competes for your attention with the spectacular rock formations, visible through the dining room's large windows; for an even better view, dine on the outside patio. The menu changes periodically, but breakfasts offer all the usuals, including a good buffet. At lunch, you'll likely find a buffet or two, plus items such as chicken salad and grilled salmon or beef burgers. Specialties at dinner might include the excellent Santa Fe flatiron steak (grilled and topped with pico de gallo and fried onions), a bison rib eye steak with a potato medley, grilled pork loin with prickly pear sauce, slow-cooked baby back ribs, plus seafood and pasta. We heartily recommend the lodge's specialty desserts, such as the bourbon pecan pie or turtle bundt cake. There is full liquor service.

Zion Lodge, Zion National Park. ℂ **435/772-7760.** www.zionlodge.com. Dinner reservations required in summer. Main courses breakfast $4–$10, lunch $8–$12, dinner $14–$29. AE, DC, DISC, MC, V. Daily 6:30–10:30am, 11:30am–3pm, and 5–10pm.

Outside the Park
SPRINGDALE

Bit & Spur Restaurant & Saloon ★★ MEXICAN/SOUTH-WESTERN   Rough wood-and-stone walls and an exposed-beam ceiling give this restaurant the look of an Old West saloon. It's actually much more than that, with a family dining room, patio dining, and original art decorating the walls. The food here is also a lot better than you'll find in the average saloon, closer to what we expect in an upscale Santa Fe restaurant. The menu changes seasonally, but usually includes Mexican standards such as burritos, flautas, chilies rellenos, and a traditional green-chile stew with pork and rice. You'll also often find seafood, such as grilled salmon, and our personal favorite, grilled chile-rubbed rib eye steak with a port wine and blue cheese demiglace. The Bit & Spur has full liquor service—try the fresh fruit margaritas—an extensive wine list, and an excellent variety of microbrewed beers.

1212 Zion Park Blvd., Springdale. (€) **435/772-3498.** www.bitandspur.com. Reservations recommended. Main courses $12–$25. AE, DISC, MC, V. Spring through fall daily 5–10pm; call for winter hours.

Spotted Dog Café ★★ AMERICAN/REGIONAL This restaurant's art-filled interior makes the most of the scenery, with large windows for inside diners plus a Euro-style outdoor patio with spectacular views of Zion Canyon. Selections vary by season and may include Rocky Mountain trout, lamb, free-range poultry, hormone-free beef, environmentally farmed fish, hearty pastas, fresh summer salads, plus local specialties. There is also a surprisingly healthy children's menu. It offers an Express Breakfast Buffet daily at 7am featuring country potatoes, bacon, link sausage, plus selections of eggs, cereal, pastries, yogurt, fresh fruit, French toast, waffles, and freshly baked specialties. The Spotted Dog has an excellent wine cellar, microbrewed draft beers, and complete liquor service.

At Flanigan's Inn, 428 Zion Park Blvd., Springdale. (€) **435/772-0700.** Reservations recommended. Main courses $12–$26. AE, DISC, MC, V. Daily 7–11am and 5–9pm; reduced hours in winter.

Zion Park Gift & Deli ★ 🍴 DELI Want a top quality sandwich at an economical price? This is the place. You can eat at one of the cafe-style tables inside or on the patio outside, or you can carry your sandwich off on a hike or to a national park picnic ground. All baked goods, including the excellent sandwich breads and sub rolls, are made in-house. In typical deli style, you order at the counter and wait as your sandwich is prepared with your choice of bread, meats, cheeses, and condiments. This is also a good breakfast stop for those who enjoy fresh-baked cinnamon rolls, muffins, banana nut bread, and similar goodies, with a cup of espresso. Locally made candy, including 14 flavors of excellent fudge, and 24 flavors of ice cream and frozen yogurt are offered. No alcohol is served.

866 Zion Park Blvd., Springdale. ✆ **435/772-3843.** $5-$10. DISC, MC, V. Summer Mon-Sat 8:30am-9:30pm; reduced hours in winter.

Zion Pizza & Noodle ★ ☺ PIZZA/PASTA   A favorite of locals and visitors, this busy cafe offers good pizza and pasta in a funky atmosphere—a former Mormon church with a turquoise steeple. The dining room has small, closely spaced tables and black-and-white photos on the walls. You find your own table, place your order at the counter, and a server delivers it. The pizzas, with lots of chewy crust, are baked in a slate stone oven. Choose one of the house favorites, such as the Southwest burrito pizza or barbecue chicken pizza, a basic cheese pizza, or create your own by adding any of the more than 20 extra toppings, from pepperoni to green chilies to pineapple. The menu also offers pastas, such as chicken parmesan, or penne pasta with grilled chicken, broccoli, carrots, fresh cream, and cheese; plus calzones and stromboli. Beer is served inside and in the delightful year-round beer garden.

868 Zion Park Blvd., Springdale. ✆ **435/772-3815.** www.zionpizzanoodle.com. Reservations not accepted. Entrees $11-$16. No credit cards. Summer daily from 4pm; call for winter hours.

OUTSIDE THE EAST ENTRANCE TO ZION NATIONAL PARK

Golden Hills Restaurant AMERICAN   There is a casual, homey atmosphere at this simply decorated and affordable family-style restaurant, where you'll find made-from-scratch breads, pies, and soups. Breakfasts include a good choice of omelets and other egg and pancake offerings; lunch is burgers and sandwiches, a soup and salad bar, plus scones with butter and honey. For dinner, you can get steak, chicken, fish, pork, and pasta. We especially recommend the country-fried steak and cream of broccoli soup. Beer and wine are served.

At the junction of Utah 9 and U.S. 89, at the Golden Hills Motel, Mt. Carmel Junction. ✆ **435/648-2602.** Reservations not accepted. Main courses lunch $4-$8, dinner $8-$20. MC, V. Summer daily 7am-10pm; winter Tues-Sun 8am-8pm.

Thunderbird Restaurant AMERICAN   You won't go wrong stopping here for basic American food at reasonable prices. The spacious dining room offers booths and tables in a comfortable, Southwest setting. The breakfast menu includes pancakes, French toast, cereal, fruit, breads, numerous egg dishes, and a hearty steak and eggs platter. Lunch consists of a wide variety of burgers plus hot and cold sandwiches. Dinner entrees include steak, seafood, and chicken, plus the popular country-fried steak. The restaurant has great homemade pies, breads, and soups, and a soup and salad bar is open at dinner in summer. Beer and wine are served.

At the junction of Utah 9 and U.S. 89, in the Best Western East Zion Thunderbird Lodge, Mt. Carmel Junction. © **435/648-2262.** Reservations not accepted. Main courses lunch $7–$14, dinner $9–$21. AE, DC, DISC, MC, V. Summer daily 7am–11pm; winter daily 7am–8pm.

EXPLORING BRYCE CANYON NATIONAL PARK

5

The scenic beauty of Bryce Canyon National Park is unsurpassed—and because it is among the West's most accessible parks, its wonders can be enjoyed by everyone from the very young to the very old, from hearty backpackers to visitors in wheelchairs. Bryce's defining feature is its hoodoos—those rock formations that delight the child in all of us. But look a bit deeper and you'll discover Bryce Canyon's other facets, from its varied wildlife to its rugged forests.

ESSENTIALS

GETTING THERE/GATEWAYS   Situated in the mountains of southern Utah, the park is crossed east-west by Utah 12, which eventually heads out of the park east to Tropic and eventually to Escalante. The bulk of the park, including the visitor center, is accessed by Utah 63, which turns south off Utah 12 into the main portions of the park. U.S. 89 runs north-south, west of the park.

VISITOR CENTER & INFORMATION   The visitor center, at the north end of the park, just after you enter (there is only one entrance, see the map on p. 70), has exhibits on the geology and history of the area and presents an excellent introductory video program on the park, which we recommend seeing if you have time. There are large photos of many of the park's better-known formations, and a relief map that shows

Bryce Canyon and nearby sections of the Colorado Plateau, including Grand Staircase–Escalante National Monument. Rangers can answer questions and provide backcountry permits; several free brochures are available; and books, maps, videos, postcards, and posters are sold. The visitor center is open daily year-round except Thanksgiving, Christmas, and New Year's Day. Summer hours are usually from 8am to 8pm, with shorter hours the rest of the year (in the dead of the winter, the visitor center will close at 4:30pm).

FEES Entry into the park (for up to 7 days) costs $25 per private car, pickup truck, van, or RV, which includes unlimited use of the park shuttle (when it's operating). Individuals 16 and older entering the park on motorcycle, bike, or foot are charged $12 each; those 15 and under are admitted free. Campsites cost $15 per night.

Backcountry permits are required for all overnight trips into the backcountry, and for up to 7 days cost $5 for one or two people, $10 for three to six people, and $15 for 7 to 15 people (group sites only). Backcountry camping is permitted on only two trails (details are available at the visitor center).

REGULATIONS & WARNINGS Hikers should practice minimum-impact techniques. All hikers are prohibited from building fires and must carry their own water, as water sources in the backcountry are unreliable. Bicycles are prohibited in the backcountry and on all trails. Feeding or disturbing wildlife, vandalism, and upsetting any natural feature of the park are all prohibited. Pets, which must be leashed at all times, are prohibited on all trails, in the backcountry, and in public buildings.

Trailers are not permitted beyond Sunset Campground; they can be left at a campsite, at the visitor center, or in other designated parking areas. Any vehicle longer than 25 feet (large trucks and motor homes, for instance) cannot go to Paria View.

While most visitors to Bryce Canyon enjoy an exciting vacation without mishap, accidents can occur, and here—possibly because of the nature of the trails—the most common injuries by far are sprained, twisted, and broken ankles. Park rangers strongly recommend that hikers—even those out on short day hikes—wear sturdy hiking boots with good traction and ankle support.

A concern in the park in recent years has been **bubonic plague,** which, contrary to popular belief, is treatable with antibiotics if caught early. The bacteria that cause bubonic plague have been found on fleas in prairie dog colonies in the park, so you should avoid contact with wild animals, especially prairie dogs and other rodents. Those taking pets into the park should dust them

Bryce Canyon National Park

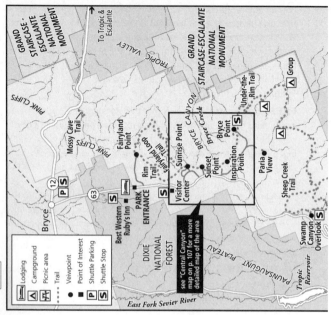

To Tropic & Escalante
GRAND STAIRCASE-ESCALANTE NATIONAL MONUMENT
PINK CLIFFS
TROPIC VALLEY
GRAND STAIRCASE-ESCALANTE NATIONAL MONUMENT
Group
Under-the-Rim Trail
Mossy Cave Trail
PINK CLIFFS
Fairyland Point
Fairyland Loop
Rim Trail
BRYCE CANYON
Sunrise Point
Bryce Creek
Bryce Point
Sunset Point
Inspiration Point
Paria View
Sheep Creek Trail
Visitor Center
PARK ENTRANCE
Best Western Ruby's Inn
Bryce
63
12
DIXIE NATIONAL FOREST
PAUNSAUGUNT PLATEAU
Swamp Canyon Overlook
Tropic Reservoir
East Fork Sevier River

see "Central Canyon" map on p. 107 for a more detailed map of the area

Legend:
Lodging
Campground
Picnic area
Trail
Viewpoint
Point of Interest
Shuttle Parking
Shuttle Stop

with flea powder. Avoiding contact with infected animals will greatly minimize the chances of contracting the plague, but caution is still necessary.

Symptoms, which generally occur from 2 to 6 days after exposure, may include high fever, headache, vomiting, diarrhea, and swollen glands. Anyone with these symptoms following a park visit should get medical attention immediately, because the plague can be fatal if not treated promptly.

TIPS FROM A PARK RANGER

Former park ranger Dave Mecham says it's easy to pinpoint Bryce Canyon's most striking feature—it's the hoodoos.

"They're photogenic, stunningly beautiful. You can find freestanding rock formations throughout the world, but I don't think there's any place where hoodoos are this numerous, this delicately eroded, or this beautifully colored." (For a discussion of the geologic forces that form hoodoos, see p. 14.)

But what Mecham enjoys most about the park is not necessarily its most recognizable feature. He prefers standing on the rim and

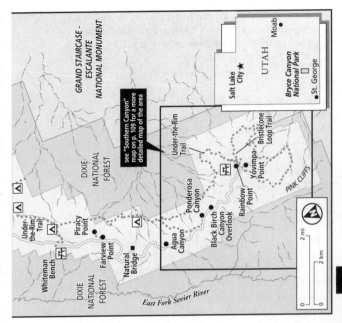

simply relishing the views: "Looking out from the rim of Bryce, across the hoodoos, it seems you can see forever. The atmospheric conditions are almost ideal, and you get the feeling that you're looking at a piece of America that's still pretty wild, and just hasn't changed much through time."

Bryce Amphitheater ★★★ has the best scenery in the park, in Mecham's opinion: "It's the place in the park where everything's coming together geologically to carve hoodoos at their best." Mecham particularly enjoys the **Rim Trail** that runs along the edge of the canyon, and highly recommends the section between Inspiration and Bryce points, with perhaps the very best view from a section known as **Upper Inspiration Point,** which is 900 to 1,200 feet south of Inspiration Point.

Among Mecham's favorite trails is the **Fairyland Loop** ★★, which takes about 4 hours. To get the best views, start at Sunrise Point, go down past Tower Bridge, and back up through Fairyland Canyon to Fairyland Trail Head. Then take the Rim Trail back to Sunrise Point. "It's 5 miles below the rim and then 3 miles of Rim Trail. Fairyland Canyon is beautiful—the highlight of that loop—and

On a hot summer day, the best spot in the park for a picnic lunch is Rainbow Point, where you'll find picnic tables and restrooms. It's also among the coolest areas because, at 9,115 feet of elevation, it's the highest point in the park.

as you come around the bend, you're hiking straight toward a really beautiful backdrop. If you're going in the opposite direction, you have to keep stopping to look over your shoulder."

Mecham calls Bryce Canyon a "morning park," because, with only a few exceptions, the views are much better illuminated by early morning light than at any other time of day. To get the most out of your visit, he recommends spending at least 1 night at or near the park: "If you're spending the night close by, I think it would be a big mistake to miss sunrise—in the middle of the summer, that's getting up before 6am."

Getting up early is also the best way to avoid crowds, according to Mecham, because most people don't get to the viewpoints or onto the trails until about 10am. The other way to avoid crowds is to walk away from them. Mecham says that you're likely not to see anyone at all on the park's two backcountry trails at the south end of the park; but avoiding crowds, even in the park's most popular areas, often takes only a short walk. "**Sunset Point** is probably the busiest place in the park, especially in midsummer at midday," he says. "You finally get a parking spot, then walk out to a very crowded viewpoint, where you're standing shoulder to shoulder—it's real hectic, but if you take a 5-minute walk south along the Rim Trail toward Inspiration Point, you'll leave the people immediately—they just cluster at those views."

Mecham says that September and October are probably the best times to visit the park. "It's still busy," he says, "but less crowded on trails." However, if you really want to avoid people, you'll feel you have the park all to yourself if you visit midweek in the middle of the winter. "We plow the roads so people can drive to the viewpoints and photograph the canyon with snow on it, and people that ski or snowshoe will enjoy it the most." He adds, "Skiing is at its best in January and February, when it's really cold."

THE HIGHLIGHTS

Everyone should spend at least a little time on the park's **scenic drive,** following the canyon rim south to Rainbow Point. There are

✑ restrooms **AT BRYCE CANYON**

The nicest and most modern restrooms at Bryce Canyon are at the visitor center and just off the lobby at the Lodge at Bryce Canyon. They're well maintained, heated, and have flush toilets and sinks with hot water.

There are also restrooms with hot water at the General Store in the park (about a quarter-mile south of North Campground, near the Sunrise Point parking area), and just outside the park entrance at Ruby's Inn (just off the lobby).

Other park facilities range from flush toilets at North and Sunset campgrounds and Sunset Point to vault toilets at Rainbow, Yovimpa, and Farview points. Although there are few toilets along trails (none in the backcountry), spring through fall, you will find a vault toilet on the Peekaboo Loop Trail, just west of its intersection with the Bryce Point cutoff trail.

Although essentially outhouses, vault toilets—officially called "bulk-reduction toilet systems"—have come a long way in the past 30 years—they're now clean, sanitary, and best of all, they don't smell. However, there is no water for hand-washing, no lights, and no heat. During busy times, the less-developed restroom facilities may run out of toilet paper, so it's best to carry a backup supply.

numerous stops where you can get off the shuttle or out of your vehicle and gaze into the canyon to view the varicolored formations. There are also numerous trail heads along the drive that provide access down into the amphitheaters. (For more information on this and other drives, see "Seeing the Park by Car," below; also check out chapter 6, "Hikes & Other Outdoor Pursuits in Bryce Canyon National Park," where you'll find detailed information on all the hiking trails and activities mentioned in this section.)

Another top experience is walking the **Rim Trail** for at least a short way, to access different views into Bryce Amphitheater, the park's largest and most colorful natural amphitheater. Although it's worthwhile at any time of day, the Rim Trail is especially wonderful just after sunrise, when you can catch the changing angles of the sun on the hoodoos.

One viewpoint not to be missed is the appropriately named **Inspiration Point ★★★**, which provides a splendid view down into Bryce Amphitheater. This viewpoint provides the best view of **Silent City,** an area that's packed with hoodoos and jump-starts the imagination. Some of us, however, believe the view is even better just south of Inspiration Point along the Rim Trail, up a little rise, at what is usually called **Upper Inspiration Point ★★★**. We think this is possibly the best view in the park.

To get a real feel for the canyon and to get grand close-up views of many spectacular formations, you must hike down into the canyon to walk among the hoodoos. One of the best canyon trails is the **Queen's Garden Trail ★★★**, which can be hiked in only a few hours, is easy enough for most park visitors—including children—and takes you to some fascinating hoodoos.

Speaking of hoodoos, there are a few of these naturally sculpted monuments in stone that are on almost everyone's must-see list. Majestic **Queen Victoria** can be seen from Sunrise Point on the rim, but is better examined from the Queen's Garden Trail. Magnificent **Thor's Hammer** is visible from Sunset Point, but is best seen from the **Navajo Loop Trail ★**.

Attractions that aren't made of stone include Bryce Canyon's **bristlecone pine trees,** exceptionally old evergreens that grow in some of the more inhospitable areas of the park. They're easily seen via the Bristlecone Loop Trail. See p. 132 for more information on these trees.

SEEING THE PARK IN 1 OR 2 DAYS

It would be easy to spend a week in Bryce Canyon, starting with the visitor center, moving along to the scenic drive, taking a few short walks, and then advancing to more serious hikes. But what makes this park so attractive is that there are ways to see a good deal of Bryce in a short amount of time.

Get an early start, stopping first at the **visitor center,** of course, where you can watch an introductory video that explains some of the area's geology—the *why* and *how* of Bryce. Then either drive the 18-mile (each way) dead-end **scenic drive** (p. 76), stopping at viewpoints to gaze down into the canyon (see "Seeing the Park by Car," below), or hop onto the **shuttle** (see "Seeing the Park by Shuttle" below), which will take you to most of the main view-

Spotting Peregrine Falcons

For a good chance to see peregrine falcons, go to Paria View, sit quietly away from the crowds, and then look out over the amphitheater, where these beautiful birds can often be spotted.

wildlife VIEWING

Bryce Canyon has a wide variety of wildlife, ranging from mule deer—which seem to be almost everywhere—to the golden-mantled ground squirrel and Uinta chipmunk. Also in the park are black-tailed jackrabbits, coyotes, striped skunks, and deer mice. Occasionally, visitors catch a glimpse of a mountain lion, most likely on the prowl in search of a mule-deer dinner. Elk and pronghorn may also be seen at higher elevations.

The Utah prairie dog, listed as a threatened species, is actually a rodent and not a distant canine relative. It inhabits park meadows in busy colonies and can be fascinating to watch. However, don't get too close because its fleas may carry disease (see "Regulations & Warnings," earlier in this chapter).

There are many birds in the park. You're bound to hear the obnoxious call of the Steller's Jays. Other birds often seen include violet-green swallows, common ravens, Clark's nutcrackers, American robins, red-shafted flickers, dark-eyed juncos, and chipping sparrows. Watch for white-throated swifts as they perform their exotic acrobatics along cliff faces. The park is also home, at least part of the year, to peregrine falcons, red-tailed hawks, golden eagles, bald eagles, and great horned owls.

The Great Basin rattlesnake, although pretty, should be given a wide berth. Sometimes growing to more than 5 feet long, this rattler is the park's only poisonous reptile. Happily, like most rattlesnakes, it is just as anxious as you are to avoid a confrontation. Other reptiles you may see are the mountain short-horned lizard, tree lizard, side-blotched lizard, and northern sagebrush lizard.

For detailed information on many of these animals, plus the various plants you'll encounter in the park, see chapter 9, "A Nature Guide to Zion & Bryce Canyon National Parks."

points. Whichever way you choose to get around, spend at least a little time at **Inspiration Point,** which offers a splendid (and yes, inspirational) view into **Bryce Amphitheater** and its hundreds of statuesque pink, red, orange, and brown hoodoo stone sculptures.

After seeing the canyon from up above, we recommend that you get some exercise by walking at least part of the way down into the canyon on the **Queen's Garden Trail.** If you can spare 3 hours, hike down the **Navajo Loop Trail ★** and return to the rim via **Queen's Garden Trail** (both are described in chapter 6, "Hikes & Other Outdoor Pursuits in Bryce Canyon National Park"). Those not willing or physically able to hike into the canyon can enjoy a leisurely walk along the **Rim Trail,** which provides spectacular views down into the canyon. In the evening, try to take in a campground amphitheater program (different programs are held in all the different campground's amphitheaters).

SEEING THE PARK BY CAR

The park's 18-mile (one-way) **scenic drive ★★** follows the rim of Bryce Canyon, offering easy access to a variety of views into the fanciful fairyland of stone sculptures below. Trailers are not permitted on the road but can be left at several parking lots. Also, because all overlooks are on your left as you begin your drive, it's best to avoid crossing traffic by driving all the way to the end of the road without stopping and then stopping at the overlooks on your return trip. Allow 1 to 2 hours for the main viewpoints, 3 to 4 hours if you plan to do a bit of walking.

From the visitor center, drive 18 miles to **Yovimpa** and **Rainbow Point** overlooks, which offer expansive views of southern Utah, Arizona, and sometimes even New Mexico. From these pink cliffs, you can look down on a colorful platoon of stone soldiers, standing at eternal attention. The short **Bristlecone Loop Trail** (p. 81), from Rainbow Point, leads to an **1,800-year-old bristlecone pine,** believed to be one of the oldest living things at Bryce Canyon. Heading north, the **Black Birch Canyon Overlook** is a roadside pullout, where you get a good view of the southern part of the park, including Rainbow Point.

From here, drive back north to **Ponderosa Canyon Overlook,** where you can gaze down at multicolored hoodoos from a dense forest of spruce and fir. Then continue to **Agua Canyon Overlook,** which has some of the best color contrasts you'll find in the park. Look almost straight down to see the **Hunter,** a hoodoo with a hat of evergreens.

Continue on to **Natural Bridge,** actually an arch carved by rain and wind, which spans 85 feet. From here, continue to **Farview Point,** where there's a panoramic view to the distant horizon and the Kaibab Plateau, at the Grand Canyon's north rim. From Farview Point, a dirt path leads several hundred feet north to **Piracy Point,** which offers good views to the north. After passing the **Swamp Canyon** overlook, continue until you see a right turn off the main road, where you'll find three viewpoints.

The first of these is **Paria View,** with views to the south of the White Cliffs, which have been carved in the light-colored sandstone by the Paria River.

To the north of Paria View, you'll find **Bryce Point ★**, a splendid stop for viewing the awesome **Bryce Amphitheater,** the largest natural amphitheater in the park. This is also a terrific point to take in distant views of the Black Mountains, to the northeast, and Navajo Mountain, to the south.

From here, it's just a short drive back toward the main road and **Inspiration Point,** a must-see stop offering views similar to those at Bryce Point, plus the best view in the park of the **Silent City,** a collection of hoodoos that looks like a sleeping city cast in stone.

Now return to the main road and head north to **Sunset Point,** where you can see practically all of Bryce Amphitheater, including the aptly named **Thor's Hammer** and the 200-foot-tall cliffs of **Wall Street.**

Continue north to a turnoff for your final stop, at **Sunrise Point ★★**, where there's an inspiring view into Bryce Amphitheater. This is the beginning of the **Queen's Garden Trail,** an excellent choice for a quick walk below the canyon's rim (p. 83).

SEEING THE PARK BY SHUTTLE

To alleviate traffic congestion during the busy summer season, a voluntary **shuttle service** runs from early May through early October, daily from 8am until 7:40pm (until 5:40pm the last few weeks of the shuttle season). Visitors can park their cars at the parking and boarding area at the intersection of the entrance road and Utah 12, 3 miles from the park boundary, and ride the shuttle into the park. Those staying in the park at the Lodge at Bryce Canyon or one of the campgrounds can also use the shuttle, at no additional charge (see "Fees," earlier in this chapter). The shuttle has stops at various viewpoints, as well as at Ruby's Inn, Ruby's Campground, the visitor center, Sunset Campground, and the Lodge at Bryce Canyon. The shuttle runs every 12 to 15 minutes and is handicap accessible. The shuttle is free and you can get on and off as you please. Note that using the shuttle is not required; you can use your own car if you wish.

HISTORIC & MAN-MADE ATTRACTIONS

Although prehistoric American Indians and 19th-century pioneers spent some time in what is now Bryce Canyon National Park, they left little evidence. The park's main historic site is the handsome sandstone and ponderosa pine **Lodge at Bryce Canyon ★★**, built by the Union Pacific Railroad, and opened in 1924. Much of it has been faithfully restored to its 1920s appearance, and the lobby contains historic photos taken in the park during that period.

RANGER & EDUCATIONAL PROGRAMS

Park rangers present a variety of free programs and activities. One-hour **evening programs,** which may include a slide show, take place at the Lodge at Bryce Canyon, the visitor center, and occasionally at the North Campground amphitheater. Topics vary, but could include such subjects as the animals and plants of the park, geology, and the role of humans in the park's early days. Rangers also give half-hour talks several times daily at various locations in the park, and lead hikes and walks, including a **moonlight hike ★★** and a wheelchair-accessible, 1.5-hour **canyon rim walk ★★** (Reservations are required, so sign up at the visitor center.) Schedules are posted on bulletin boards at the visitor center, General Store, campgrounds, and the Lodge at Bryce Canyon.

Especially popular are the park's **Astronomy Programs ★**, which are usually offered 3 nights a week through the summer. Telescopes are provided.

The **High Plateaus Institute,** which is affiliated with Bryce Canyon Natural History Association, occasionally presents educational programs for the public. For details, check with park offices

---

🗨 Bryce Canyon in Outer Space

In 2007, the International Astronomical Union approved the naming of minor planet 49272 as **Bryce Canyon.** There are hundreds of thousands of minor planets—most of us call them asteroids—ranging in size from several yards across to hundreds of miles across. The Bryce Canyon asteroid, estimated to be 3 to 5 miles across, orbits the Sun between Mars and Jupiter, but is too dim to be seen by the naked eye or even with a small telescope.

---

or the Bryce Canyon Natural History Association (℃ **888/362-2642** or 435/834-4782; www.brycecanyon.org).

GUIDED TOURS

For a bird's-eye view of the canyon and its numerous formations, contact **Bryce Canyon Airlines & Helicopters** (℃ **435/834-8060;** www.rubysinn.com/bryce-canyon-airlines.html) for scenic flights by helicopter or open cockpit bi-plane. Tours last from about 35 minutes to several hours, and the longer trips include surrounding attractions. Prices start at about $100 per person, and reservations are required.

Several national **adventure tour operators** offer guided biking, hiking, and backpacking trips near the park, and other companies offer more traditional tour packages (p. 162).

ESPECIALLY FOR KIDS

Bryce Canyon is a fantasyland that kids love—even teenagers trying their hardest to be bored will have a great deal of trouble not being fascinated by the bizarre and whimsical stone shapes that are the essence of this park. Among the best trails for kids are **Queen's Garden Trail** ★★★ and **Navajo Loop Trail** ★, which are not only fairly easy, but lead to some of the park's best hoodoos. Teenagers with a bit more stamina will probably enjoy the 8-mile **Fairyland Loop.** Details on all the hikes are available in the "Day Hikes" section of chapter 6.

During the summer, children can join the **Junior Rangers,** participate in a variety of programs, and earn free patches. Junior Rangers booklets are available at the visitor center. In addition, park rangers periodically conduct **special kids' activities**—usually lasting about an hour—on subjects such as the park ecology. Reservations are required; contact the visitor center for information.

HIKES & OTHER OUTDOOR PURSUITS IN BRYCE CANYON NATIONAL PARK

One of the wonderful things about Bryce Canyon is that even though hiking is the best way to explore it, you don't have to be an advanced backpacker to really get to know the park. There are ample opportunities to experience much of the park on easy walks, and many people see the park from the back of a mule or horse. In the winter, the park's trails are open to snowshoers and cross-country skiers.

Several national adventure tour operators offer guided hiking, backpacking, and biking trips in and near the park; see "Package & Adventure Tours," in chapter 162.

DAY HIKES

Remember that all trails below the rim have at least some steep grades, so you should wear hiking boots with a traction tread and good ankle support to avoid ankle injuries, the most common accidents in the park. During the hot summer months, you'll want to hike

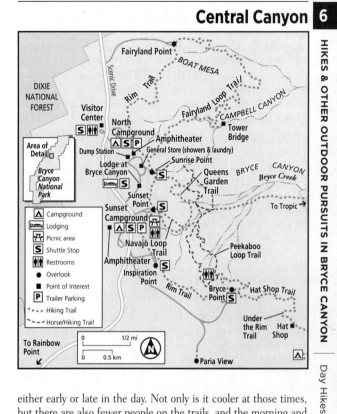

either early or late in the day. Not only is it cooler at those times, but there are also fewer people on the trails, and the morning and late afternoon lighting on the hoodoos can produce dramatic effects. Bryce's rangers have recently stopped rating hiking trails as to their difficulty, saying that what is easy for one person may be difficult for another. Ratings here are provided by the authors and other experienced hikers, and are entirely subjective.

Note: "RT" stands for round-trip in the following trail listings.

Shorter Hikes

Bristlecone Loop Trail ★★ ☺ Especially pleasant on a hot day, this is an easy walk through a forest of shady evergreens. Entirely above the canyon rim, the trail winds among white fir, Douglas fir, and ponderosa and bristlecone pines; you'll see more bristlecones here than on any other park trail. More than many other species, the bristlecone can withstand the strong winds and harsh conditions often found on high ridges, as well as times of prolonged drought; consequently, they often live to a great age— one in California is more than 4,000 years old! The oldest bristlecone pines in Bryce Canyon are nearly 2,000 years old. The trail has an elevation change of 150 feet, and the round-trip takes about an hour. See map on p. 83.

1 mile RT. Easy. Access: The trail head is located at the Rainbow Point parking area at the end of the scenic drive.

Hat Shop Trail   This is a strenuous hike with a 1,336-foot elevation change; it's also the beginning of the **Under the Rim Trail** (see "Exploring the Backcountry," later in this chapter). Leaving the rim, you'll drop quickly to the Hat Shop, so-named because it consists of a series of rock formations that resemble hard gray hats perched on narrow, reddish-brown pedestals. The trail offers close-up views of gnarled ponderosa pine and Douglas fir, as well as distant panoramas across the Aquarius Plateau toward the Grand Staircase–Escalante National Monument. (See chapter 8, "Nearby Things to See & Do.") This hike will take you approximately 4 hours, if you go the whole distance. See map on p. 81.

4 miles RT. Difficult. Access: The trail head is located at the Bryce Point Overlook.

Mossy Cave Trail ★ 🎒   An often-overlooked trail, located outside the main part of the park, the Mossy Cave Trail offers an easy and picturesque walk. The trail follows an old irrigation ditch up a short hill to a shallow cave, where seeping water nurtures the cave's namesake moss. Just off the trail, you'll see a small waterfall, which is usually flowing from May through October. Elevation gain is 200 feet. Allow about 45 minutes for the whole trip.

.8 mile RT. Easy. Access: The trail head is located along Utah 12, about 3½ miles east of the park access road, Utah 63.

📎 The Best of Two Great Trails

A great choice for getting down into the canyon and seeing the most scenery with the least amount of sweat is to combine **Navajo Loop Trail** with the **Queen's Garden Trail**. The total distance is just under 3 miles, and most hikers take from 2 to 3 hours to make the hike. It's best to start at the Navajo Loop Trail Head at Sunset Point and leave the canyon on the less steep Queen's Garden Trail, returning to the rim at Sunrise Point, a half-mile north of the Navajo Loop Trail Head.

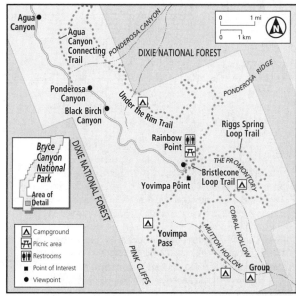

Navajo Loop Trail ★   This trail descends from the canyon rim 550 feet to the bottom of the canyon floor and back up again. Traversing graveled switchbacks, it affords terrific views of several impressive formations, including the awesome Two Bridges and the precariously balanced Thor's Hammer. The round-trip on this trail takes 1 to 2 hours, and we suggest hiking the trail clockwise. See map on p. 81.

1.3 miles RT. Moderate. Access: The trail head is signposted at the central overlook at Sunset Point.

Queen's Garden Trail ★★★   This short trail, which drops 320 feet below the rim, takes you down into Bryce Amphitheater, with rest benches near the formation called **Queen Victoria.** At the beginning of the descent, keep an eye cocked to the distant views so you won't miss Boat Mesa, the Sinking Ship, the Aquarius Plateau, and Bristlecone Point. As you plunge deeper into the canyon, the trail passes some of the park's most fanciful formations, including majestic Queen Victoria herself (the formation looks like a full-figure profile of the British monarch), for whom the trail and this grouping of hoodoos are named, plus the Queen's

HOODOO PHOTOGRAPHY: THE "light" STUFF

The delightful rock formations that decorate the amphitheaters at Bryce Canyon National Park beg to be photographed, and they have been—many times and from every conceivable angle. Look at those expensive, glossy calendars or the various coffee-table books filled with dramatic photos of the American West. In almost every single publication of this kind, you'll see Bryce Canyon's hoodoos standing tall, with their vibrant reds and oranges set against a pure blue sky and accented by the rich greens of junipers and piñon.

This scenery is why you came, and among the best souvenirs you can take home are good quality photos that you've taken yourself. While at Bryce Canyon, you're apt to see photographers loaded down with expensive equipment and all manner of lenses and filters; although these tools can be helpful (and fun), the most important element of photography is not the equipment, but the photographer. The way to get good photos of Bryce Canyon's hoodoos with practically any type of camera is simple: Choose your timing for the best lighting—usually sunrise—compose carefully, and keep your camera steady.

Professional photographers are always carrying on about getting the right light, and at Bryce Canyon this is especially important. That's because of the nature of the hoodoos. In early morning (and to a somewhat lesser degree in late afternoon), the low angle of the sun brings out the richness of the rocks' colors—especially the reds and oranges—and emphasizes shadows, creating a multi-dimensional scene. On the other hand, around noon, with light coming straight down, the hoodoos look washed out and flat.

Choosing a photographing location isn't difficult. There are plenty of spots along the Rim Trail for early-morning shots; those looking for sunset photos should head down the Rim Trail, past Inspiration Point, where it climbs a small hill, for the best angles. Those with telephoto or zoom lenses have the advantage of being able to get a variety of shots from one location along the rim; for close-ups and unique angles, you'll want to hike below the rim, and a wide-angle lens will often produce the best results. Some photographers like to use polarizing filters to bring out the colors of the rocks and deepen the blue of the sky.

A tripod is useful, especially when the light is a bit dim, to minimize vibration and help keep the camera from moving while you find the right composition. Those without tripods can steady their cameras by folding or balling up a jacket or sweater, resting it on a railing or other solid object, and holding the camera against it.

Castle and Gulliver's Castle. The round-trip takes 1 to 2 hours. See map on p. 81.

1.8 miles RT. Moderate. Access: The trail head is located on the south side of Sunrise Point.

Longer Hikes

Fairyland Loop Trail ★   A good choice for a challenging hike that offers panoramic vistas away from the crowds, from Fairyland Point this little-traveled trail descends into Fairyland Canyon, then meanders up, down, and around Boat Mesa. It crosses Campbell Canyon, passes Tower Bridge junction—a short, 600-foot side trail takes you to the base of Tower Bridge—and begins a steady climb to the China Wall. About halfway along the wall, the trail begins the serious ascent back to the top of the canyon, which it reaches near Sunrise Point. To complete the loop, follow the Rim Trail back through juniper, manzanita, and Douglas fir to Fairyland Point, a trip that will take you approximately 5 hours. The loop has an elevation change of about 2,309 feet. See map on p. 81.

8 miles RT. Difficult. Access: The trail head is located at the Fairyland Point Overlook, off the park access road north of the visitor center; the trail is also accessible from Sunrise Point.

Peekaboo Loop Trail ★   This trail, open both to those on foot and on horseback, winds among hoodoos below Bryce and Inspiration points. It's a steep and strenuous hike, with an elevation change of 1,555 feet. You follow the Under the Rim Trail briefly toward the Hat Shop, but soon you'll turn left and head toward the Peekaboo Loop. This section of the trail is narrow and often littered with rocks, so place your feet carefully. Fairly steep inclines and descents alternate with more level stretches; stop frequently to take in both the close and distant vistas. At times you can see far to the east beyond Bryce Canyon toward the Aquarius Plateau, Canaan Mountain, and the Kaiparowits Plateau; you'll get closer views of the unusual Wall of Windows, the Three Wise Men, the Organ, and the Cathedral. Various connecting trails make Peekaboo easily accessible. There's a corral and vault toilets toward the Bryce Point end of the loop. The park's horseback-ride concessionaire uses the trail

Beating the Heat

The lower you drop below the rim, the hotter it gets; so carry water and dress in layers that can be easily removed and carried as the temperature rises.

spring through fall, and hikers should step aside to let horseback riders through. Hiking the entire trail takes 3 to 4 hours. See map on p. 81.

5.5 miles RT. Difficult. Access: The trail head is located at the Bryce Point Overlook parking area.

Rim Trail ★★★ ☺ The Rim Trail, which does not drop into the canyon, offers splendid views from above, giving us the whole picture of this phenomenal spectacle of carved stone. More of a walk than a hike, the trail includes a .5-mile section between two overlooks—Sunrise and Sunset—that is paved, fairly level, and suitable for wheelchairs. Overlooking Bryce Amphitheater, the trail offers almost continually excellent views as it meanders along the rim, and is a good choice for an early morning or evening walk, when you can watch the changing light on the rosy rocks below. Another advantage is that you can access the trail from many locations, so you can have a short or long walk. You may also find this a convenient trail if you just want to rush out to the rim for a quick look at sunrise over the hoodoos. Some people feel that the absolute best view in the park is from the Rim Trail, south of Inspiration Point. If you do the whole thing, which most people don't, it's a maximum of 5 to 6 hours with a total elevation change of 1,734 feet. See map on p. 81.

11 miles RT. Easy to moderate. Access: The northern trail head is at Fairyland Point; the southern trail head is at Bryce Point. The trail is also accessible from Sunrise, Sunset, and Inspiration points, and numerous other locations in between.

Sheep Creek Trail This trail takes you down into the canyon bottoms, and, if you continue, right out of the park into the Dixie National Forest. The first mile is on the rim; then the trail descends along Sheep Creek draw and meanders below pink limestone cliffs toward the canyon bottom, traversing part of the Under the Rim Trail along its way. Watch signs carefully; the route can be confusing. The trail has up to a 1,250-foot elevation change, and it will take you about 5 hours if you go just to the park boundary, 8 hours if you go to the end.

6–10 miles RT (3 miles takes you to the park boundary and another 2 miles brings you to the national forest boundary). Easy to moderate. Access: The trail head sign and parking area are 5 miles south of the visitor center, on the scenic drive.

EXPLORING THE BACKCOUNTRY

For diehard hikers who don't mind rough terrain, Bryce has two backcountry trails, usually open in the summer only. The really ambitious can combine the two for a week-long excursion. Permits, which are available at the visitor center, are required for all overnight trips into the backcountry. Cost is $5 for one or two people, $10 for three to six people, and $15 for 7 to 15 people (group sites only). Permits cannot be reserved, but must be obtained at the park during the 48 hours preceding your hike. Although the number of permits issued is limited, park officials say they seldom run out. Permits can be obtained daily from 8am until 1 hour before the visitor center closes.

Riggs Spring Loop Trail ★★   This hike can be completed in 4 or 5 rigorous hours, or it can be more comfortably done as a relaxing overnight backpacking trip. This relatively little-used trail offers a good opportunity to escape humanity. You'll have a good chance of seeing wildlife—possibly even a glimpse of an elusive mountain lion. (See chapter 9, "A Nature Guide to Zion & Bryce Canyon National Parks.") The trail goes through a deep forest of Douglas fir and ponderosa pine early on, and then turns south through a burned-out area, past blackened trees and brush to the brink of the Pink Cliffs, where you can gaze into a valley of hoodoos below. Yovimpa Pass Campground, about 2 miles into the hike, occupies a tree-rimmed meadow with views of Molly's Nipple and No Man's Mesa. The descent from Yovimpa Pass follows the bed of Podunk Creek, crossing the wash several times, and traversing a forest of ponderosa and piñon pines, aspen, Douglas fir, and manzanita, before turning toward Riggs Spring and the Riggs Spring Campground (3.4 miles from the trail head). The spring is on the west side of the trail and is encircled by a wood rail fence. The trail next turns north, following Mutton Hollow and crossing several washes, finally arriving at Corral Hollow Campground, at the base of the Promontory, just beyond a small stand of maple trees. (You've come 5.7 miles at this point.) The trail now begins the loop around the Promontory, sometimes crossing draws that provide clear views of the white and pink cliffs soaring above. Once around the southern tip of the promontory, the trail begins the steady return ascent to the rim of the canyon. The elevation change of the hike is 2,248 feet. See map on p. 83.

8.5 miles RT. Moderate to difficult. Access: The trail head is located on the south side of the parking area for Rainbow Point.

Under the Rim Trail   Running just below the rim between Bryce and Rainbow points, the Under the Rim Trail has numerous fairly steep inclines and descents, with an overall elevation change of 1,500 feet. There are five camping areas along the route, plus a group camp area. Doing this whole trail should take you 2 to 3 days.

Although the trail doesn't move too far from the scenic drive, its location below the rim gives hikers a feeling of being alone in the wilderness. There are several spurs connecting this trail to the scenic drive, which enables hikers to choose a route to match their abilities and time schedule. The **Sheep Creek Trail** (9.5 miles from the trail head) and **Swamp Canyon Connecting Trail** (10.4 miles from the trail head) both lead to the Swamp Canyon Overlook and parking area on the scenic drive. **Whiteman Connecting Trail** (12.3 miles from the trail head) takes hikers to a picnic area on the scenic drive; and **Agua Canyon Connecting Trail** (16.9 miles from the trail head) connects to Ponderosa Canyon Overlook and parking area on the scenic drive. Plan carefully, because once you choose your route it is written on your overnight pass and you cannot change your campsite.

From Bryce Point, the trail meanders toward Merrell Hollow across almost-empty meadows that are home to an occasional twisted conifer and a few manzanita. Nearing the hollow you'll see chipmunks darting about gathering food, and you'll have grand vistas of the Aquarius Plateau, with Tropic Valley nestled in the foreground. The pinnacles grouped at the head of the hollow are brilliantly painted in purples, reds, and oranges. As you descend a long slope, you'll see the Hat Shop ahead. (See "Hat Shop Trail," earlier in this chapter.) Continuing the descent, you'll finally arrive at Right Fork Camping Area (3 miles from the trail head), located in a tall stand of ponderosa pines.

From Right Fork, the trail follows a deep wash through low brush to Yellow Creek, which it follows upstream, passing the Yellow Creek Group Camp (4 miles from the trail head). As you continue upstream, you'll spot desert shrubs and barrel cactus among the junipers. (See chapter 9, "A Nature Guide to Zion & Bryce Canyon National Parks.") In the occasional spaces between the trees, you can see the colorful spires at the top of the valley. Near the stream source is the Yellow Creek Camping Area (5.4 miles from the trail head), located in a grove of tall pines; shortly after you leave the campground, the trail climbs a slope with grand views to the east, where gray cliffs provide a backdrop for deep red formations of sandstone.

The trail next passes through open pine forests, along washes, and up and down valleys, offering varying views of carved and etched walls, square-topped pillars, and a mountain topped with sharp pinnacles. Rock cairns (conical heaps of stone) mark the trail when it begins to fade. Once across the Sheep Creek Trail and wash, you'll wind around, up, and then down into the Swamp Canyon bottoms, where cool air pools and aspens grow. After the Right Fork Swamp Canyon Camp (10.5 miles from the trail head), you'll climb onto the top of the plateau, pass an amphitheater filled with lovely hoodoos, and arrive at Swamp Canyon Camp (12.2 miles from the trail head), high above the canyon floor.

As you continue, the trail heads in a southerly direction, descending into the upper basin of Willis Creek, climbing into a sandy saddle, and then descending into Bridge Canyon—look to the west for a clear view of Natural Bridge. Once in the canyon bottom, the trail arrives at Bridge Canyon Camp (15.6 miles from the trail head), nestled among pine trees. Although cliffs are visible from the campground, the Natural Bridge is blocked from view.

After crossing an open meadow that's blanketed with a profusion of yellow wildflowers in late summer, you'll follow Agua Canyon upstream—rock cairns help keep you on course. As you approach the head of the wash, you'll start up a steep, north-facing incline partially shaded with Douglas fir. As you near the crest, the trees thin out, providing magnificent views north and west.

Dropping into the next basin, you pass under a colorful cliff, after which the trail climbs several ridges and skirts a bowl filled with hoodoos, before arriving at the small Iron Spring Camping Area (19.5 miles from the trail head). Next you'll climb a gradual but constant slope toward the rim, with increasingly panoramic views of the orange cliffs north to Bryce Point. Soon a turn to the west blocks this vista, and you have a steep climb to achieve the rim and the Rainbow Point parking area—the end of the trail, where you'll find a picnic area and restrooms. Rainbow Point is also the trail head for the Bristlecone Loop (described earlier in this chapter) and Riggs Spring Loop trails (above). See map on p. 83.

22.9 miles one-way. Moderate to difficult. Access: The trail head is located on the east side of the parking area for Bryce Point Overlook.

OTHER SUMMER SPORTS & ACTIVITIES

BIKING Bikes are prohibited on all trails, and are forbidden from traveling cross-country within the national park boundaries. The park's established scenic drive is open to road or mountain bikers, although you need to be aware that the 18-mile road through the park is narrow and winding, and can be crowded with motor vehicles during the summer.

Because mountain bikers are not welcome on national park hiking trails, you'll have to leave Bryce in search of trails. Fortunately, you won't have to go far—the **Dixie National Forest,** which abuts the park, has numerous mountain biking opportunities. (See chapter 8, "Nearby Things to See & Do.")

Mountain bikes can be rented across the road from Ruby's Inn at the **Bryce Canyon American Car Care Center** (✆ **866/866-6616** or 435/834-5232; www.rubysinn.com) for $20 for up to 6 hours and $35 for a full day.

FISHING   The closest fishing hole to the park is at **Tropic Reservoir** in the Dixie National Forest. (See chapter 8, "Nearby Things to See & Do.")

HORSEBACK RIDING   To see Bryce Canyon the way the early pioneers did, you need to look down from a horse. **Canyon Trail Rides,** P.O. Box 128, Tropic, UT 84776 (✆ **435/679-8665;** www.canyonrides.com), offers a close-up view of Bryce's spectacular rock formations from the relative comfort of a saddle. The company has a desk inside Bryce Lodge. A 2-hour ride to the canyon floor and back costs $50 per person, and a half-day trip farther into the canyon costs $75 per person. Rides are offered April through November. Riders must be at least 7 years old for the 2-hour trip, at least 10 for the half-day ride, and weigh no more than 220 pounds.

Horseback rides are also offered by several companies in Red Canyon, just outside the national park. See the Dixie National Forest section in chapter 8.

WINTER ACTIVITIES

Bryce is beautiful in the winter, when the white snow creates a perfect frosting on the red, pink, orange, and brown statues standing proudly against the cold winds.

CROSS-COUNTRY SKIING   Cross-country skiers will find several marked, ungroomed trails (all above the rim), including the **Fairyland Loop Trail** ★★, which leads 1 mile through a pine and juniper forest to the Fairyland Point Overlook. From here you can take the 1-mile **Forest Trail** back to the road, or continue north along the rim for another 1.2 miles to the park boundary.

There are also connections to ski trails in the adjacent national forest. (See "Dixie National Forest," in chapter 8.)

Stop at the visitor center for trail information, and go to **Best Western Plus Ruby's Inn,** just north of the park entrance (✆ **866/866-6616** or 435/834-5341; www.rubysinn.com), for information on cross-country ski trails and snowmobiling opportunities outside the park. Ruby's grooms over 30 miles of ski trails, some of which connect to trails within the national park, and also rents cross-country ski equipment.

Winter Safety

Although the entire park is open to cross-country skiers, rangers warn that it's extremely dangerous to try to ski on the steep—and often slick—trails leading down into the canyon.

SNOWSHOEING Snowshoeing is allowed anywhere in the park except on cross-country ski tracks. There are also numerous areas outside the park that are suitable for snowshoeing. Snowshoes can be rented at **Ruby's Inn.** (See "Cross-County Skiing," above.)

WHERE TO STAY, CAMP & EAT IN BRYCE CANYON

7

Although you don't have as many choices for lodging, eating, and camping inside Bryce Canyon National Park as you do at larger parks, such as Yosemite and Grand Canyon, to our thinking, what is offered at the Lodge at Bryce Canyon is a perfect complement to your national park experience. In addition to being well managed, the lodge and park campgrounds offer incredible views and a rustic, rugged, mountain atmosphere that can't be beat.

However, let's not put down the facilities available in the nearby gateway communities. Here you'll find a variety of lodging and dining choices, often at lower prices than inside the park, as well as campgrounds with RV hookups and all the other amenities that are lacking in the national park campgrounds.

WHERE TO STAY

Room tax adds about 11% to your lodging bill. Pets are not accepted unless otherwise noted.

For additional information on area lodging, contact **Bryce Canyon Country,** operated by the Garfield County Office of Tourism (© **800/444-6689** or 435/676-1102; www.brycecanyoncountry.com).

We offer one note of caution. Communities and facilities as much as an hour away from the park boast that they are the best places to stay when visiting Bryce Canyon. We disagree.

Although you can often find attractive facilities at very reasonable rates by driving far from the park, we don't think it's worth it. For one thing, you will spend too much time, energy, and money to get here to waste time commuting.

Perhaps more important, though, is that Bryce Canyon is especially delightful early and late in the day; and the closer you are to the park, the more likely you are to be on the rim for the spectacular sunrise and sunset colors.

All of the properties discussed here are in or near the park.

Inside the Park

The Lodge at Bryce Canyon ★★★ This sandstone and ponderosa pine lodge, which opened in 1924, offers the perfect atmosphere for visiting Bryce Canyon National Park. The lodge provides extremely close access to the Rim Trail, the ideal spot for watching the play of changing light on the rock formations.

The luxurious lodge suites are wonderful, with white wicker furniture, ceiling fans, and separate sitting rooms. The motel units are simply pleasant modern motel rooms, with two queen-size beds and either a balcony or a patio. Our choice is one of the historic cabins, restored to their 1920s appearance. They're a bit small, but have two double beds, high ceilings, stone (gas-burning) fireplaces, and log beams—you might call the ambience "rustic luxury." The gift shop has one of the best selections of American Indian jewelry in the area. All units are nonsmoking.

Bryce Canyon National Park, (P.O. Box 640041), Bryce, UT 84764. www.bryce canyonforever.com. (✆ **877/386-4383** or 435/834-8700. 114 units (110 in motel rooms and cabins; 3 suites and 1 studio in lodge). $130–$165 double; $175 cabin; $179 lodge suite. AE, DISC, MC, V. Closed Mid-Nov through Mar. **Amenities:** Restaurant (p. 100).

Outside the Park
TROPIC & BRYCE

See chapter 8, "Nearby Things to See & Do," for a discussion of things to see and do in these gateway communities.

Best Western Plus Bryce Canyon Grand Hotel ★★ This upscale hotel, which opened in 2009, offers excellent facilities just a stone's throw from the entrance to Bryce Canyon National Park. The rooms and suites, contained in two four-story towers with interior corridors, are what we call "Western luxury," with solid wood furnishings, good lighting, and top quality beds—either one king or two queens. The hotel caters to those who want to take care of business while on vacation, with large working desks plus everything else you might want to keep in touch with the office. The large deluxe suites, at 770 square feet each, have a king bed, hide-a-bed couch, and jetted tub. The hotel is under the same management as the nearby Best Western Plus Ruby's Inn (see below). All units are non-smoking.

31 N. 100 E. (at the entrance to Bryce Canyon), Bryce Canyon City, UT 84764. www.brycecanyongrand.com. © **866/866-6634** or 435/834-5700. Fax 435/834-5701. 162 units. Summer $150 double, $200–$290 suite; rest of year $75 double, $140–$199 suite. Rates include a hot breakfast. AE, DC, DISC, MC, V. **Amenities:** Restaurant; fitness center; heated outdoor pool (May–Oct only); whirlpool. In room: A/C, TV, fridge, hair dryer, microwave, Wi-Fi.

Best Western Plus Ruby's Inn ★★ ☺

Most of the tired hikers and canyon rim gazers visiting the park stay at this large motel, and with good reason—not only is Ruby's among the closest lodgings to the park, but the lobby is among the busiest places in the area, with tour desks where you can arrange excursions of all sorts, from horseback and all-terrain-vehicle rides to helicopter flights.

Spread among nine buildings, the modern motel rooms contain art that depicts area scenery, wood furnishings, and tub/shower combos. Deluxe units, located in the main building, have either jetted tubs or two-person jetted spas. Rooms at the back of the complex will be a bit quieter, but farther from the lobby. There is also a campground on the property. (See "Camping," below.) All units are nonsmoking.

26 S. Main St. (at the entrance to Bryce Canyon), Bryce Canyon City, UT 84764. www.rubysinn.com. © **866/866-6616** or 435/834-5341. 370 units. June–Sept $135–$169 double, $195 suite; Oct–May $70–$140 double, $145 suite. AE, DC, DISC, MC, V. Pets accepted ($20 per night fee). **Amenities:** 2 restaurants (Canyon Diner and Cowboy's Buffet and Steak Room; see reviews, p. 101); concierge; indoor heated pool; 1 indoor and 1 outdoor whirlpool; general store; liquor store; photo shop; U.S. Post Office. In room: A/C, TV, fridge, microwave, hair dryer, Wi-Fi.

Bryce Canyon Pines

A modern motel with a Western flair, the Bryce Canyon Pines offers well-maintained rooms with light-colored wood furnishings and two queen-size beds in most rooms. Some units have fireplaces (wood supplied free), some have kitchenettes, and one has its own whirlpool tub. A family suite contains one king-size bed plus two queen-size beds, each in a separate room. There are also some rustic cottages. All units have private bathrooms with tub/shower combos. You can book horseback rides from Red Canyon Trail Rides (p. 107) and trail ride/lodging packages here. All units are nonsmoking. There is also a campground on the property. (See "Camping," below.)

Milepost 10, Utah 12 (3 miles west of intersection with park entry road; P.O. Box 640043), Bryce, UT 84764. www.brycecanyonmotel.com. © **800/892-7923** or

435/834-5441. Fax 435/834-5330. 53 units. $55–$105 double, $95–$130 cottages, $120–$325 deluxe rooms & suites; highest rates are in summer. AE, DC, DISC, MC, V. **Amenities:** Restaurant adjacent (see review, p. 100); covered heated pool (Apr–Oct only); whirlpool. *In room:* A/C, TV, Wi-Fi.

Bryce Country Cabins ★★ There's something special about staying in a genuine log cabin during a national park vacation, but there's also something very appealing about hot showers and warm beds. Bryce Country Cabins offers the best of both worlds, with modern log cabins and a historic pioneer cabin. The grounds are nicely landscaped, with good views, although we wish the units were farther from the highway.

The modern cabins have knotty pine walls and ceilings, exposed beams, and ceiling fans. Each has one or two queen-size beds, a table and chairs, and a porch. Bathrooms have shower/tub combos or showers only. The 1905 pioneer cabin has two spacious rooms with country-style decor. Each has two queen-size beds and full bathroom, and the rooms can be rented together or individually. There are outdoor barbecues, a fire pit for evening gatherings, and a children's play-fort. All cabins are nonsmoking.

320 N. Utah 12 (P.O. Box 141), Tropic, UT 84776. www.brycecountrycabins.com. ⓒ **888/679-8643** or 435/679-8643. 13 units. Summer $95–$135 double; lower rates at other times. AE, DC, MC, V. *In room:* A/C, TV, fridge, hair dryer, microwave, Wi-Fi.

Bryce Pioneer Village Motel This is a good choice for those seeking a good night's rest at a reasonable rate. Decor is simple, with light-colored walls and rustic touches like rough log headboards in some units. The small, no-frills motel rooms are clean and comfortable, with one or two queen-size beds or two double beds, large walk-in closets, and showers only (no tubs). Cabins, relocated from inside the national park, are more interesting. Most are small but cute, with one queen-size bed, one chair, and a small bathroom with shower. Several others are larger, with two queen-size beds and average-size bathrooms with tub/shower combinations. There are also cabins with three queen-size beds or one queen and a kitchenette. Just outside the office is the cabin where Ebenezer and Mary Bryce, for whom the park is named, lived in the late 1870s. There is also a campground on the property (p. 98).

80 S. Main St. (Utah 12; P.O. Box 119), Tropic, UT 84776. www.brycepioneervillage. com. ⓒ **866/657-8414** or 435/679-8546. Fax 435/679-8607. 62 units. Summer $65–$80 double, $70–$90 cabins and kitchenette units; winter rates lower. DISC, MC, V. **Amenities:** 2 whirlpool tubs; picnic area. *In room:* A/C, TV, Wi-Fi.

Bryce Valley Inn A member of the America's Best Value Inn & Suites franchise, the Bryce Valley Inn offers simply decorated, basic motel rooms that are a clean, well-maintained, and relatively economical choice for park visitors. Units are furnished with either one king-size bed, one or two queen-size beds, or two double beds. There are also suites with either one queen or one king bed, plus a refrigerator and microwave. All units are nonsmoking. A gift shop on the premises offers a large selection of American Indian arts and crafts, handmade gifts, rocks, and fossils.

199 N. Main St., Tropic, UT 84776. www.brycevalleyinn.com. (*) **800/442-1890** or 435/679-8811. 65 units. Late spring to early fall $85–$115 double and suite; rates from $50 double the rest of the year. AE, DISC, MC, V. 8 miles east of the park entrance road. Pets accepted ($20 fee). **Amenities:** Restaurant. *In room:* A/C, TV, Wi-Fi.

Bryce View Lodge ★ 🏷 This basic modern American motel gets our vote for the best combination of economy and location. It consists of four two-story buildings, set back from the road and grouped around a large parking lot and attractively landscaped area. The simply decorated average-size rooms are comfortable and quiet, with two queen-size beds and tub/shower combos. The light-colored walls help make the rooms feel larger than they are, and the rooms are decorated with artwork depicting the rock formations you'll see in the park, located just down the road. Guests have access to the amenities at Ruby's Inn, across the street. All units are nonsmoking.

105 E. Center St., Bryce Canyon City, UT 84764. www.bryceviewlodge.com. (*) **888/279-2304** or 435/834-5180. Fax 435/834-5181. 160 units. Summer $80–$110 double; rest of year $60–$100 double. AE, DC, DISC, MC, V. Pets accepted ($20 per night fee). **Amenities:** See Best Western Plus Ruby's Inn, p. 94. *In room:* A/C, TV, Wi-Fi.

Stone Canyon Inn ★★★ 📷 This charming inn is the best place to stay outside the park for those who seek upscale accommodations and fantastic views. Each room is unique, with queen or king-size beds, colorful quilts, handsome wood furnishings, and a classic Western look. Three rooms have double whirlpool tubs and separate showers, two rooms have whirlpool tub/shower combos, and one room, partly crafted for travelers with disabilities, has a traditional tub/shower combo. The four cottages—they're much too nice to call cabins—have two bedrooms and two bathrooms, gas fireplaces, full kitchens, living rooms with TVs with VCR/DVD players, tile floors, private decks with hot tubs, and barbecue grills. The inn sits well off the main road, on the boundary of the Bryce Canyon National Park, and large windows afford views either into the park or nearby Grand Staircase–Escalante National Monument. Smoking is not permitted.

1220 W. 50 S. (P.O. Box 156), Tropic, UT 84776. www.stonecanyoninn.com. (*) **866/489-4680** or 435/679-8611. From Utah 12 in Tropic, take Bryce Way Rd.

WHERE TO STAY, CAMP & EAT IN BRYCE CANYON

west 1 mile to Fairyland Lane, and follow the sign to the inn. 10 units. Apr–Oct $145-$200 rooms, $330 cottages; winter rates lower. Room rates include full breakfast; cottage rates do not. AE, DC, DISC, MC, V. Children 4 and under not allowed in the inn; no age restrictions for cottages. *In room:* A/C, TV, Wi-Fi.

CAMPING

Pets are accepted at all of the following campgrounds, but they must be leashed.

Inside the Park

The two campgrounds at Bryce are typical of campgrounds in the West's national parks, offering plenty of trees for a genuine "forest camping" experience. On the other hand, facilities are limited. **North Campground ★★★** has 101 sites and **Sunset Campground ★★** has 102 sites. Both are open to tent and RV campers. Sunset Campground is open late spring through early fall only, while a section of North Campground is open year-round. Although we would happily camp at either campground, we prefer North Campground because it's closer to the Rim Trail, making it easier to rush over to catch those amazing sunrise and sunset colors. Get to the park early to claim a site (usually by 2pm in the summer). Reservations are available from early May through late September for North Campground (© **877/444-6777;** www.recreation.gov) and for 20 tent-only sites in Sunset Campground, for an additional nonrefundable booking fee of $10. See the "Amenities for Each Campground Near & In Bryce Canyon National Park" chart, on p. 98, for more information on both campgrounds.

Showers ($2) and a coin-operated laundry, open from 7am to 8pm, are located at the **General Store** (for information, contact the Lodge at Bryce Canyon; © **435/834-5361**), which is a healthy walk from either campground. The park service operates an RV dump station ($2 fee) in the summer.

Outside the Park

Just north of the entrance to the park is **Ruby's Inn RV Park & Campground ★★**, 300 S. Main St., Bryce Canyon City, UT 84764 (© **866/878-9373** or 435/834-5301; www.rubysinn.com), which is situated just outside the park, along the shuttle bus route. The RV and tent sites are mostly shady and attractive. The campground contains an outdoor heated swimming pool, hot tub, barbecue grills, coin-operated laundry, and a store with groceries, RV supplies, and propane. A lake and a horse pasture are nearby. Also on the grounds are several camping cabins ($56 double) and

Amenities for Each Campground Near &

CAMPGROUND	ELEV.	TOTAL SITES	RV HOOKUPS	DUMP STATION	TOILETS	DRINKING WATER
Bryce Canyon Pines	7,600	39	26	no	yes	yes
Bryce Pioneer Village	6,400	32	12	yes	yes	yes
King Creek (USFS)	7,900	37	no	yes	yes	yes
Kodachrome	5,800	27	4	yes	yes	yes
North	7,700	101	no	no	yes	yes
Red Canyon (USFS)	7,240	37	no	yes	yes	yes
Ruby's Inn RV Park	7,600	250	200	yes	yes	yes
Sunset	8,000	102	no	no	yes	yes

teepees ($34 double), which share the campground's bathhouse and other facilities. See the "Amenities for Each Campground Near & In Bryce Canyon National Park" chart, above, for more information.

Bryce Pioneer Village, 80 S. Main St. (Utah 12; P.O. Box 119), Tropic, UT 84776 (© 866/657-8414 or 435/679-8546; fax 435/679-8607; www.brycepioneervillage.com), is a small motel/cabins/campground combination in nearby Tropic, with easy access to several restaurants. See the "Amenities for Each Campground Near & In Bryce Canyon National Park" chart, above, for more information.

Bryce Canyon Pines ★, milepost 10, Utah 12 (P.O. Box 640043), Bryce, UT 84764 (© 800/892-7923 or 435/834-5441; fax 435/834-5330; www.brycecanyonmotel.com), is part of a motel/restaurant/store/campground complex, about 3 miles west of the park entrance road. The campsites, set back from the highway, behind a gas station and store, are interspersed among ponderosa pines and junipers, with wildflowers and grasses. All RV sites have full hookups. Campers have access to the motel swimming pool across the street. See the "Amenities for Each Campground Near & In Bryce Canyon National Park" chart, above, for more information.

King Creek Campground ★, in the Dixie National Forest, above Tropic Reservoir, offers a quiet, peaceful forest camping experience relatively close to the national park. For information, stop at or contact the **Red Canyon Visitor Center** (© 435/676-2676), along Utah 12, about 10½ miles west of the Bryce Canyon National Park entrance road (usually open daily from early May to

In Bryce Canyon National Park

Showers	Fire Pits/ Grills	Laundry	Reserve	Fees	Open
yes	yes	yes	yes	$20–$30 Apr–Oct	Mar–Oct
yes	no	no	yes	$12–$30	Mid-May to Sept
no	yes	no	no	$12	Year-round
yes	yes	no	yes	$16–$25	Year-round
no	yes	no	yes	$15	mid-May to Sept
yes	yes	no	no	$15	Apr–Oct
yes	yes	yes	yes	$25–$41	Early May–late Sept
no	yes	no	no	$15	Apr–Oct

early October), or contact the **Dixie National Forest Information Center,** 345 E. Riverside Dr., St. George, UT 84790 (© **435/688-3246;** www.fs.fed.us/dxnf). The campground has graded gravel roads and tent and RV sites nestled among tall ponderosa pines, and the nearby reservoir has a boat ramp. (See "Dixie National Forest" in chapter 8, "Nearby Things to See & Do.") To get to the campground from the park, head north 3 miles on Utah 63, then west on Utah 12 about 2½ miles to the access road, turn south (left) and follow signs to Tropic Reservoir for about 7 miles to the campground. There is a $5 fee for use of the dump station. See the "Amenities for Each Campground Near & In Bryce Canyon National Park" chart, above, for more information.

About 9½ miles west of the park is another Dixie National Forest campground, **Red Canyon Campground ★★** (same contact as King Creek Campground, above). Nestled among the trees along the south side of Utah 12, the tent and RV sites offer terrific views of the red rock formations across the highway, although there is a bit of road noise. There are a number of scenic trails close by. Showers cost $2 and use of the dump station costs $5, whether you're staying in the campground or not. See the "Amenities for Each Campground Near & In Bryce Canyon National Park" chart, above, for more information.

Kodachrome Basin State Park, about 22 miles southeast of the park, has an attractive tent and RV campground with sites scattered among unusual rock chimneys and piñon and juniper trees. (See chapter 8, "Nearby Things to See & Do.") See the "Amenities for Each Campground Near & In Bryce Canyon National Park" chart, above, for more information.

WHERE TO EAT

In addition to the restaurants discussed below, **Ebenezer's Barn & Grill,** part of the huge Best Western Plus Ruby's Inn complex, at 26 South Main St., in Bryce Canyon City, offers a Western dinner and show, nightly at 8pm, during the summer. Similar to chuck wagon dinners elsewhere, diners go through a chow line and pick up their grub and then head to large tables to eat and enjoy the show, a combination of Western-style music and humor. Dinner choices include rib eye steak, baked salmon, baked chicken, and barbecue, with prices from $26 to $32, and all meals include beans, potatoes, corn bread, dessert, and a nonalcoholic beverage. Tickets are available at Ruby's Inn; for information call ✆ **435/834-5341 ext. 7099.**

Additional information on where to eat is available from **Bryce Canyon Country,** operated by the Garfield County Office of Tourism (✆ **800/444-6689** or 435/676-1102; www.brycecanyon country.com).

Inside the Park

Picnickers can stock up at the small General Store inside the park or at one of the several stores not far from the park entrance. See the Fast Facts entry for "Supplies" in chapter 10, "Fast Facts."

The Lodge at Bryce Canyon ★★ AMERICAN We would come here just for the mountain-lodge atmosphere, with two handsome stone fireplaces and large windows looking out on the park. But the food's good, too, and reasonably priced considering that this is the only real restaurant in the park. The service is good, although not always speedy, but this is not a fast-food restaurant. Breakfasts offer typical American standards and a good buffet. At lunch, you'll find sandwiches, burgers, salads, and a taco bar. The menu changes periodically, but may include dinner specialties such as pan-seared Alaskan sockeye salmon topped with sun-dried tomato pesto, and perhaps a rack of lamb. Steaks are also offered, including a bison tenderloin, and other dishes frequently available include chicken with lime and chile. There are also vegetarian items, and the restaurant serves wine and beer.

Bryce Canyon National Park. ✆ **435/834-8700.** www.brycecanyonforever.com. Main courses $5–$12 breakfast and lunch, $13–$25 dinner. AE, DC, DISC, MC, V. Daily 7–10am, 11:30am–3pm, and 5–10pm. Closed Mid-Nov through Mar.

Outside the Park
TROPIC & BRYCE

Bryce Canyon Pines ★ 🍴 AMERICAN A country cottage–style dining room, with an old wood stove, is the perfect setting for the wholesome American food served here. Especially popular for its traditional breakfasts, the restaurant is also known for its home-made soups and pies—all the usuals, plus some not-so-usual selections such as banana blueberry. Both sandwiches and full dinners are available at lunch and dinner. Recommended are the Utah trout; the 8-ounce tenderloin steak; and the hot sandwiches, such as the open-faced turkey with mashed potatoes and gravy. Beer and wine are available.

Utah 12, about 3 miles west of intersection with park entry road. © **435/834-5441.** www.brycecanyonmotel.com. Sandwiches $5–$12; full dinners $10–$22. AE, DC, DISC, MC, V. Daily 7am–9:30pm summer (call for hours at other times).

Canyon Diner ☺ AMERICAN   Part of the Best Western Plus Ruby's Inn complex, this self-serve restaurant offers typical fast-food fare, relatively quick and close to the park. Breakfasts, served until 11am, include bagels and several egg croissants; for lunch and dinner, you can get hoagies, burgers, hot dogs, nachos, pretty good stuffed potatoes, pizza, broiled chicken sandwiches, and salads. Specialties include a fish and chips basket. No alcohol is served.

At the Best Western Plus Ruby's Inn, 1000 S. Utah 63, Bryce Canyon City. © **435/834-8030.** www.rubysinn.com. Reservations not accepted. Individual items $4–$7; meals $6–$11. AE, DISC, MC, V. Daily 6:30am–9:30pm. Closed Nov–Mar.

Cowboy's Buffet and Steak Room STEAK/SEAFOOD   The busiest restaurant in the Bryce Canyon area, this main restaurant at the Best Western Plus Ruby's Inn moves 'em through with buffets at every meal, plus a well-rounded menu and friendly service. The breakfast buffet offers more choices than you'd expect, with scrambled eggs, fresh fruit, several breakfast meats, potatoes, pastries, and cereals. At the lunch buffet, you'll find country-style ribs, fresh fruit, salads, soups, vegetables, and breads; while the dinner buffet features charbroiled thin-sliced rib-eye steak and other meats, pastas, potatoes, and salads. Regular menu dinner entrees include prime rib, pot roast, grilled rainbow trout, grilled turkey breast, southern-style catfish, and salads. In addition to the large, Western-style dining room, an outdoor patio is open in good weather. Full liquor service is available.

At the Best Western Plus Ruby's Inn, 26 S. Main St., Bryce Canyon City. © **435/834-5341.** www.rubysinn.com. Reservations not accepted. Breakfast and lunch $3.50–$15; dinner main courses and buffets $12–$30. AE, DC, DISC, MC, V. Summer daily 6:30am–10pm; winter daily 6:30am–9pm.

Foster's Family Steak House STEAK/SEAFOOD   The simple Western decor here provides the right atmosphere for a down-to-earth steakhouse. Locally popular for its slow-roasted prime rib and steamed Utah trout, Foster's also offers several steaks (carnivores like us appreciate the 14-oz. T-bone), sandwiches, a soup of the day, and homemade chili with beans. All of the pastries, pies, and breads are baked on the premises. Bottled beer is available with meals.

At Foster's Motel, 1150 Utah 12, about 1½ miles west of the park entrance road. © **435/834-5227.** www.fostersmotel.com. Main courses $5-$12 breakfast and lunch, $12-$26 dinner. AE, DISC, MC, V. Mar–Nov daily 7am–10pm; call for winter hours.

NEARBY THINGS TO SEE & DO

T he area surrounding Zion and Bryce Canyon National Parks offers a smorgasbord of scenic wonders and recreational opportunities. The gateway communities to the parks provide a variety of activities along with a welcome change of pace for kids who might be getting a bit tired of the beautiful but seemingly endless rock formations. Adjacent to Bryce Canyon National Park is Grand Staircase–Escalante—a vast, stark, but stunningly beautiful national monument—as well as Dixie National Forest, a popular spot for mountain bikers, anglers, campers, and hikers. Within 90 minutes of the south entrance to Zion National Park, you can wander through the mysterious lava caves of Snow Canyon, or strike out off-road in a dune buggy at Coral Pink Sand Dunes State Park—and that's just for starters. Two other state parks, Kodachrome Basin and Escalante, are within an hour of the entrance to Bryce Canyon and provide lovely vistas and quirky pleasures all on their own.

GATEWAY TOWNS

Just outside the parks are communities offering additional outdoor recreation opportunities. Additional information is provided in the chapters covering activities in each of the parks.

Outside Zion National Park

The small community of **Springdale,** with a population of about 600 and an elevation of 3,900 feet, was settled in 1862 and today is the south gateway to Zion National Park. Springdale is a good spot to pick up those forgotten supplies.

HOW'S this FOR GUN CONTROL?

In response to fears that the right of U.S. citizens to own firearms was under attack, the small town of Virgin, Utah, about 15 miles west of the main entrance to Zion National Park, passed a law that required—yes, *required*—that there be a gun and ammunition in every home. The ordinance, approved in late 2000, exempted residents who could not afford to buy a gun or had moral objections, as well as those who were mentally ill or convicted felons. The town's mayor said there was a lot of support from the town's residents, most of whom already owned guns. The courts eventually struck down the law, but at least we know how the folks in Virgin feel about gun control.

The community of **Virgin** (pop. 550) lies about 13 miles west of Springdale along Utah 9. First named Pocketville because of the red sandstone cliffs that closely surround it, the town was renamed for the Virgin River that runs through it. The Kolob Terrace Road heads north out of Virgin into Zion National Park, accessing several backcountry trails.

For additional information about the area, contact the **Zion Canyon Visitors Bureau** in Springdale (© **888/518-7070;** www. zionpark.com).

Hiking, rock climbing, and mountain biking are popular activities around Springdale, and several local companies can provide advice, equipment rentals, and guided tours. (See chapter 3, "Hikes & Other Outdoor Pursuits in Zion National Park.")

The **Tanner Twilight Concert Series** presents a varied performing arts program in the stunning, 2,000-seat outdoor **Tanner Amphitheater,** just off Zion Park Boulevard. Performances range from symphony orchestra concerts and dance performances to rock, jazz, and gospel concerts. Shows begin at 8pm many Saturdays throughout the summer, and cost $10 for adults and $5 for youths (18 and younger). For information, contact **Dixie College,** in St. George (© **435/652-7994;** www.dixie.edu/tanner/index.html).

The **Zion Canyon Theatre,** 145 Zion Park Blvd. (© **888/256-3456** or 435/772-2400; www.zioncanyontheatre.com), boasts a huge screen—some 60 feet high by 82 feet across. Here you can see the dramatic film *Zion Canyon: Treasure of the Gods,* with thrilling scenes of the Zion National Park area, including a hair-raising flash flood through Zion Canyon's Narrows and some dizzying bird's-eye views. The theater also shows a variety of other Hollywood and large-format films. Admission is $8 adults and $6 children under 12. The theater is open daily from 11am in summer; call for winter hours. The theater complex also contains a tourist information center, an ATM, a picnic area, gift and souvenir shops, restaurants, and a grocery store.

Outside Bryce Canyon National Park

Just outside the entrance to Bryce Canyon National Park are the communities of **Tropic** (population 475), along Utah 12, about 8 miles east of the park entrance road, and **Bryce Canyon City** (population 140), along the entrance road and near its intersection with Utah 12. Much of the lodging, dining, and other services for park visitors can be found in these communities.

For additional information on area attractions, contact **Bryce Canyon Country,** operated by the Garfield County Office of Tourism (© **800/444-6689** or 435/676-1102; www.brycecanyon country.com).

There are a variety of outdoor activities in the Dixie National Forest (discussed below).

The **Best Western Plus Ruby's Inn** (p. 94), in Bryce, is practically a one-stop entertainment center for those looking for a bit of variety in their national park vacation.

Directly across Utah 63 from the inn are **Old Bryce Town Shops,** open daily 8am to 10pm from May through September, where you'll find a rock shop and a variety of other stores offering an opportunity to buy that genuine cowboy hat you've been wanting. There's a trail here especially for kids, where they can search for arrowheads, fossils, and petrified wood; or perhaps they would prefer checking out the jail.

Nearby, **Bryce Canyon Country Rodeo** (© **866/782-0002**) showcases bucking broncos, bull riding, calf roping, and all sorts of rodeo fun in a 1-hour program, from Memorial Day weekend through late August, Wednesday through Saturday evenings at 7pm. Admission is $10 for adults, $7 for children 3 to 12, and free for children 2 and under. Adventurous visitors can also ride: bulls for adults and steers and sheep for kids. Call for details.

DIXIE NATIONAL FOREST

Adjacent to Bryce Canyon National Park

The Dixie National Forest wraps around two-thirds of Bryce Canyon National Park: All down the west side, around the south end, and about halfway up the east side. There are a variety of outdoor activities in the forest—hiking, mountain biking, fishing, camping, and cross-country skiing. Bryce Canyon National Park's Sheep Creek Trail connects with trails in the national forest. The climate and seasons here are similar to those in Bryce Canyon National Park. (See chapter 10, "Planning Your Trip to Zion & Bryce Canyon National Parks.") Most of the areas and trails discussed below are at elevations between 7,000 and 8,000 feet.

Essentials

INFORMATION & VISITOR CENTERS   Stop at the Dixie National Forest's **Red Canyon Visitor Center** (© 435/676-2676), along Utah 12, about 10½ miles west of the Bryce Canyon National Park entrance road. It's usually open daily from early May to early October, and offers various interpretative programs on many Saturdays. Or contact the **Dixie National Forest Information Center,** 345 E. Riverside Dr., St. George, UT 84790 (© 435/688-3246; www.fs.fed.us/dxnf).

CAMPING   King Creek Campground, above Tropic Reservoir, has graded gravel roads and sites nestled among tall ponderosa pines (p. 98). About 9½ miles west of the park is **Red Canyon Campground,** named for its vermilion-colored rock formations (p. 99).

Sports & Activities

FISHING   The closest fishing hole to Bryce Canyon National Park is at **Tropic Reservoir,** in Dixie National Forest, which is a large lake in a ponderosa pine forest. From the national park entrance road, drive west about 3 miles on Utah 12 to a gravel road, turn left (south), and go about 7 miles. There's good fishing for rainbow, brook, and cutthroat trout, although some locals say fishing is sometimes better in streams above the lake than in the lake itself. Day use at the lake is free. There is also a Forest Service campground open in the summer and a boat ramp. *Note:* The boat ramp is not useable during low water periods, so check with the Red Canyon Visitor Center (see above) before dragging your boat there.

HIKING   There are about a dozen trails in the Red Canyon area of the park, and a free map is available at visitor centers. (See information above, under "Information & Visitor Centers.") Some trails are open to hikers only; others are also open to mountain bikers, equestrians, and those with all-terrain vehicles. One especially scenic multiuse trail is the 5.5-mile (one-way) **Casto Canyon Trail,** which runs along the bottom of Casto Canyon. It connects with the 8.9-mile (one-way) **Cassidy Trail** (legend has it that outlaw Butch Cassidy used this trail) (see "Butch Cassidy Slept Here," chapter 1) and the 2.9-mile (one-way) **Losee Canyon Trail** to produce a loop of about 17 miles that is ideal for a backpacking trip of several days. Watch for elk in the winter, and pronghorns and raptors year-round. The Casto Canyon and Losee Canyon trails are considered moderate, while Cassidy Trail ranges from easy to strenuous. **Sheep Creek Trail** (p. 86) connects the national forest to Bryce Canyon National Park.

For a quick, scenic walk, take the 1-mile **Pink Ledges Trail** that starts just outside the Red Canyon Visitor Center, at the east end of the parking lot. Rated moderate because of a few steep inclines, the trail has several signs discussing trees and plants, and good views of surrounding hoodoos. The only downside is that you can't escape the road noise from Utah 12.

HORSEBACK RIDING   If you've brought your own horse, you'll have a number of riding opportunities on the forest's multi-use trails. Those without horses of their own can still explore Red Canyon on horseback with **Red Canyon Trail Rides** (✆ 800/892-7923; www.redcanyontrailrides.com), with offices at Bryce Canyon Pines (p. 94). Trail rides are offered spring through fall, weather permitting, with rates of $15 for a half-hour, $30 for 1 hour, $50 for 2 hours, $65 for a half-day, and $75 to $100 for a full day, including a box lunch. Minimum age is 6 for the half- and 1-hour rides, 7 for the 2-hour and half-day rides, and 9 for the full-day rides. Advance reservations are requested.

Guided horseback rides in Red Canyon are also provided by **Ruby's Inn Horse Rides** (✆ 866/782-0002 or 435/834-5341; www.horserides.net), at Ruby's Inn. Rates are $45 for a 1-hour ride, $75 to $85 for a half-day ride, and $125 for a full day, including lunch. Ruby's will also board your horse. (Call for rates.)

MOUNTAIN BIKING   There are numerous opportunities for mountain biking in the national forest, but only on roads and specified trails. A particularly popular route is **Dave's Hollow Trail,** where you'll have a fairly good chance of seeing pronghorn and mule deer. The trail, also open to ATVs, starts at the Bryce Canyon National Park boundary sign on Utah 63, the park entrance road, about 1 mile south of Ruby's Inn. The double-track trail goes west for about half a mile before connecting with Forest Road 090, where you turn south and ride for about three-quarters of a mile before turning right onto an easy ride through Dave's Hollow to the Dave's Hollow Forest Service Station, on Forest Road 087. From here, you can retrace your route for an 8-mile round-trip

8

NEARBY THINGS TO SEE & DO

Dixie National Forest

ride; for a longer 12-mile loop, turn right on Forest Road 087 to Utah 12, and then right again back to Utah 63 and the starting point. A third option is to turn left on Forest Road 087 and follow it about 6 miles to Tropic Reservoir. (See "Fishing," above.) This part of the journey does not form a loop, so you would turn around once you've reached the reservoir.

The **Casto Canyon Trail,** in Red Canyon, is an especially scenic trail open to hikers, mountain bikers, and those on horseback. (See "Hiking," above.)

Mountain bikes can be rented across the road from Ruby's Inn at the **American Car Care Center** (✆ **866/866-6616** or 435/834-5232; www.rubysinn.com) for $20 for up to 6 hours and $35 for a full day.

WINTER ACTIVITIES   Cross-country skiing and snowshoeing opportunities abound along trails and old roads in the national forest, and snowmobiling is also popular. **Best Western Plus Ruby's Inn** (p. 94) grooms over 30 miles of cross-country ski trails for skating and classical skiing, and also rents equipment. Call for current rates.

Ruby's also offers sleigh rides when there is sufficient snow. Thirty-minute rides ($25 per person 4 and older, free for those under4) are scheduled at 9:30am, 11am, 1pm, and 2:30pm.

CEDAR BREAKS NATIONAL MONUMENT

85 miles N of the main section of Zion National Park; 56 miles W of Bryce Canyon National Park

A delightful little park, Cedar Breaks is a wonderful place to spend anywhere from a few hours to several days, gazing down from the rim into the spectacular natural amphitheater, hiking the trails, and camping among the spruce and fir trees.

This natural coliseum, which reminds us of Bryce Canyon, is more than 2,000 feet deep and over 3 miles across; it's filled with stone spires, arches, and columns painted in ever-changing reds, purples, oranges, and ochers. But why "Cedar Breaks"? Well, the pioneers who came here called such badlands "breaks," and they mistook the juniper trees along the cliff bases for cedars.

Essentials

At over 10,000 feet of elevation, it's always pleasantly cool at Cedar Breaks. It actually gets downright cold at night, so bring a jacket or sweater, even if the temperature is scorching just down the road in St. George. The monument is open to those traveling by car, truck, or RV for a short summer season—from after the snow melts, usually in late May, until the first heavy snow, usually in mid-November. However, if you have a snowmobile or a pair of cross-country skis or snowshoes, you can visit throughout the winter.

GETTING THERE From Zion National Park, head west on Utah 9, then north on Utah 17 to I-15. Follow the interstate north to exit 57 for Cedar City, and head east on Utah 14 to Utah 148. Turn north (left), and follow Utah 148 into the monument. If you're coming from Bryce Canyon, which is 56 miles east of the monument, or other points east, the park is accessible from the town of Panguitch via Utah 143. If you're traveling from the north, take the Parowan exit off I-15 and head south on Utah 143. It's a steep climb from whichever direction you choose, and vehicles prone to vapor lock or loss of power on steep hills (such as RVs) may have some problems.

INFORMATION/VISITOR CENTER A mile from the south entrance gate, you'll find the **visitor center,** which is usually open daily from late May through mid-October, daily from 9am to 6pm (closed the rest of the year). The visitor center has exhibits on the geology, flora, and fauna of Cedar Breaks. You can purchase books and maps here, and rangers can help you plan your visit. For advance information, contact **Cedar Breaks National Monument,** 2390 W. Utah 56, Ste. 11, Cedar City, UT 84720 (© **435/ 586-9451** (administrative office) or 435/586-0787 (monument office, open in summer only; www.nps.gov/cebr).

FEES & REGULATIONS Admission for up to 1 week, charged only from late May through mid-October, costs $4 per person for all those 16 and older, free for those 15 and under. Admission is free the rest of the year. Regulations are similar to those at most national parks: Leave everything as you find it. Mountain bikes are not allowed on hiking trails. Dogs, which must be leashed at all times, are prohibited on all trails, in the backcountry, and in public buildings.

CAMPING The 28-site campground, **Point Supreme,** just north of the visitor center, is usually open from mid-June through late September, with tent, car, and RV sites available on a first-come, first-served basis. The campground is in a beautiful high-mountain setting, among tall spruce and fir. Facilities include restrooms, drinking water, picnic tables, grills, and an amphitheater for the rangers' evening campfire programs. No showers or RV hookups are available. Camping fee is $14 per night. Keep in mind that even in midsummer, temperatures can drop into the 30s (low single digits Celsius) at night at this elevation, so bring cool-weather gear.

Cedar Breaks National Monument

HEALTH & SAFETY CONCERNS The high elevation—10,350 feet at the visitor center—is likely to cause shortness of breath and tiredness, and those with heart or respiratory conditions should consult their doctors before visiting. Avoid high, exposed areas during thunderstorms—they're often targets for lightning.

RANGER PROGRAMS During the monument's short summer season, rangers offer campfire talks at the Point Supreme campground several nights a week, daily talks on geology and other subjects, and several guided hikes. There are also special programs on the monument's wildflowers, and, in recent years, stargazing programs have become especially popular. All ranger programs are free. A complete schedule is posted at the visitor center and the campground.

Exploring Cedar Breaks by Car

The 5-mile road through Cedar Breaks National Monument offers easy access to the monument's scenic overlooks and trail heads. Allow 30 to 45 minutes to make the drive. Start at the visitor center and nearby **Point Supreme** for a panoramic view of the amphitheater. Then drive north, past the campground and picnic ground turnoff, to **Sunset View,** for a closer view of the amphitheater and its colorful canyons. From each of these overlooks, you'll be able to see out across Cedar Valley, over the Antelope and Black mountains, into the Escalante Desert.

Continue north to **Chessman Ridge Overlook,** so named because the hoodoos directly below look like massive stone chess pieces. Watch for swallows and swifts soaring among the rock formations. Then head north to **Alpine Pond,** a trail head for a self-guided nature trail with an abundance of wildflowers. (See "Hiking," below.) Finally, you'll reach **North View,** which offers your best look into the amphitheater. The view here is reminiscent of Bryce Canyon's Queen's Garden, with its stately statues frozen in time.

Sports & Activities

HIKING The fairly easy 2-mile round-trip **Alpine Pond Nature Trail** loop leads through woodlands of bristlecone pines to a picturesque forest glade and a pond surrounded by wildflowers, offering panoramic views of the amphitheater along the way. A trail guide pamphlet is available at the trail head.

A somewhat more challenging hike, the 4-mile round-trip **Spectra Point/Ramparts Overlook Trail** follows the rim more closely than the Alpine Pond Trail, offering changing views of the colorful

The Summer Wildflowers of Cedar Breaks

During its brief summer season, Cedar Breaks makes the most of the warmth and moisture in the air with a spectacular wildflower show. The rim comes alive in a blaze of color—truly a sight to behold. The dazzling display begins practically as soon as the snow melts and reaches its peak in mid-July. The annual 2-week **Wildflower Festival,** which celebrates the colorful display, starts the weekend closest to Independence Day. Watch for mountain bluebells, spring beauty, beard tongue, and fleabane early in the season; those beauties then make way for columbine, larkspur, Indian paintbrush, wild roses, and other flowers.

rock formations. It also takes you through fields of wildflowers and by bristlecone pines that are more than 1,600 years old. You'll need to be especially careful of your footing along the exposed cliff edges, and allow yourself some time to rest—there are lots of ups and downs along the way.

The 1-mile round-trip **Campground Trail** connects the campground with the visitor center, providing views of the amphitheater along the way. It is the only trail in the monument where pets are permitted.

There are no trails from the rim to the bottom of the amphitheater completely within the monument, but there are trails just outside the monument that go into the amphitheater. Check with the visitor center for details and directions.

WILDLIFE-WATCHING   Because of its relative remoteness, Cedar Breaks is a good place for spotting wildlife. You're likely to see mule deer grazing in the meadows along the road early and late in the day. Marmots make their dens near the rim and are often seen along the Spectra Point Trail. You'll spot ground squirrels, red squirrels, and chipmunks everywhere. Pikas, which are related to rabbits, are here, too, but it's unlikely you'll see one. They're small, with short ears and stubby tails, and prefer the high, rocky slopes.

Also look for birds, such as swallows, swifts, blue grouse, and golden eagles, and watch for Clark's nutcrackers, with their gray torsos and black-and-white wings and tails.

WINTER ACTIVITIES   The monument's facilities are usually shut down from mid-November to late May due to the thick blanket of snow that covers it. The snow-blocked roads keep cars out, but they're perfect for snowmobilers, snowshoers, and cross-country skiers, who usually come over from nearby Brian Head ski area. Note that snowmobiles are restricted to the main 5-mile road through the monument, which is groomed and marked.

GRAND STAIRCASE-ESCALANTE NATIONAL MONUMENT

59 miles E of Bryce Canyon National Park (to the town of Escalante)

Covering almost 1.9 million acres, this vast area of red-orange canyons, mesas, plateaus, and river valleys is known for its stark, rugged beauty. Operated by the Bureau of Land Management (BLM), it contains a unique combination of geological, biological, paleontological, archaeological, and historical resources.

In announcing the creation of the monument from lands already under federal control in 1996, former President Bill Clinton proclaimed, "This high, rugged, and remote region was the last place in the continental United States to be mapped; even today, this unspoiled natural area remains a frontier, a quality that greatly enhances the monument's value for scientific study."

While hailed by environmentalists, the president's action was not popular in Utah, largely because the area contains a great deal of coal and other valuable resources. Utah Senator Orrin Hatch denounced Clinton's decree, calling it "the mother of all land-grabs."

Unlike most other national monuments, practically all of this vast area is undeveloped—there are few all-weather roads, only one maintained hiking trail, and two developed campgrounds. But the adventurous will find miles upon miles of dirt roads and what are called "hiking routes," offering practically unlimited opportunities for hiking, horseback riding, mountain biking on existing dirt roads, and camping.

The national monument can be divided into three distinct sections: The **Grand Staircase** of sandstone cliffs, which includes five life zones, from Sonoran Desert to coniferous forests, in the southwest; the **Kaiparowits Plateau,** a vast, wild region of rugged mesas and steep canyons, in the center; and the **Escalante River Canyons** section, along the northern edge of the monument, a delightfully scenic area containing miles of interconnecting river canyons.

Essentials

Over such a vast area, weather conditions vary greatly, but it's safe to say that summers are hot. As with most parts of southern Utah, spring and fall are the best times to visit.

Grand Staircase–Escalante National Monument

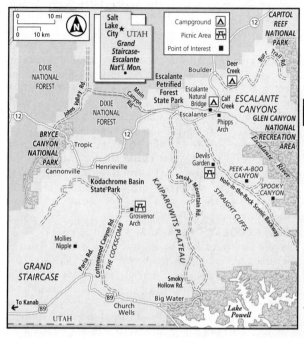

0 ——— 10 mi	Campground △
0 ——— 10 km	Picnic Area 🏕
	Point of Interest ■

Salt Lake City ★ UTAH
Grand Staircase-Escalante Nat'l. Mon. ■

DIXIE NATIONAL FOREST

Escalante Petrified Forest State Park

Boulder

Deer Creek △

CAPITOL REEF NATIONAL PARK

Burr Trail Rd.

Johns Valley Rd.
Main Canyon Rd.

DIXIE NATIONAL FOREST

Escalante Natural Bridge △
Calf Creek ■

ESCALANTE CANYONS

Escalante

Phipps Arch ■

GLEN CANYON NATIONAL RECREATION AREA

Escalante River

BRYCE CANYON NATIONAL PARK
Tropic

Henrieville
Cannonville

Kodachrome Basin State Park

Devils Garden 🏕

PEEK-A-BOO CANYON ■

Hole-in-the-Rock Scenic Backway

SPOOKY CANYON ■

Smoky Mountain Rd.

STRAIGHT CLIFFS

KAIPAROWITS PLATEAU

Grosvenor Arch

Cottonwood Canyon Rd.
THE COCKSCOMB
Paria Rd.

Mollies Nipple ■

GRAND STAIRCASE

Smoky Hollow Rd.

To Kanab ←
89

89

Church Wells

Big Water

Lake Powell

UTAH

GETTING THERE The national monument occupies a large section of southern Utah—covering an area almost as big as the states of Delaware and Rhode Island combined—with Bryce Canyon National Park to the west, Capitol Reef National Park on the northeast edge, and Glen Canyon National Recreation Area along the east and part of the south sides.

Access is via Utah 12, along the monument's northern boundary, from Kodachrome Basin State Park and the communities of Escalante and Boulder; and via U.S. 89 to the southwestern section of the monument, east of the town of Kanab, which is about 80 miles south of Bryce Canyon.

INFORMATION & VISITOR CENTERS The national monument remains a very rugged area, with limited facilities, poor roads, and changeable weather. To put it bluntly, people die here, so we strongly recommend that before setting out, all visitors contact one of the monument's visitor centers to get maps and other information, and especially to check on current road and weather conditions. Also see the monument's website, **www.ut.blm.gov/monument**.

Visitor centers include the **Escalante Interagency Visitor Center,** on the west side of Escalante, at 755 W. Main St. (Utah 12), Escalante, UT 84726 (© **435/826-5499**), open daily 8am to 4:30pm from mid-March through mid-November, and Monday through Friday the same hours the rest of the year. You can also get information at the Bureau of Land Management's **Kanab Visitor Center,** 745 E. U.S. 89, Kanab, UT 84741 (© **435/644-4680**), open daily 8am to 4:30pm.

The **Cannonville Visitor Center** is open daily from 8am to 4:30pm, mid-March through mid-November only, at 10 Center St., in Cannonville (© **435/826-5640**), east of Bryce Canyon National Park. The **Big Water Visitor Center** is along U.S. 89, near the southern edge of Glen Canyon National Recreation Area, at 100 Upper Revolution Way, in Big Water (© **435/675-3200**). It is open daily from 9am to 5:30pm April through October and daily 8am to 4:30pm the rest of the year.

FEES, REGULATIONS & SAFETY There is no charge to enter the monument; however, those planning overnight trips into the backcountry must obtain free permits at any of the visitor centers listed above. Regulations are similar to those on other public lands, but damaging or disturbing archaeological and historic sites in any way is particularly forbidden. There are also several areas where dogs are forbidden; check with one of the visitor centers.

Water is the main safety concern here—either too little or too much. This is generally very dry country, so carry plenty of drinking water. However, thunderstorms can turn the monument's dirt roads into impassable mud bogs in minutes, stranding motorists; and potentially fatal flash floods through narrow canyons can catch hikers by surprise. Anyone planning trips into the monument should check first with one of the offices listed above for current and anticipated weather and travel conditions, and should be alert to changing conditions while exploring the monument.

Grand Staircase–Escalante National Monument

NEARBY THINGS TO SEE & DO

Impressions

On this remarkable site, God's handiwork is everywhere.
—President Bill Clinton, September 18, 1996

CAMPING   There are two designated campgrounds in the monument. **Calf Creek Campground,** in the Calf Creek Recreation Area, about 15 miles northeast of the town of Escalante via Utah 12, has 14 sites and a picnic area. Open year-round, the tree-shaded campground is situated in a scenic, steep canyon along Calf Creek, surrounded by high rock walls. Facilities include picnic tables, grills, and an interpretive hiking trail. (See "Hiking, Mountain Biking & Horseback Riding," below.) There also are flush toilets and drinking water, but no showers, RV hookups, RV dump station, or trash removal. In summer, the campground is often full by 10am. November through March, water is turned off and only vault toilets are available. Vehicles must ford a shallow creek, and the campground is not recommended for vehicles over 25 feet long. Campsites cost $7 per night; day use is $2 per vehicle.

The national monument's other designated campground is **Deer Creek,** located 6 miles east of the town of Boulder along the scenic Burr Trail Road. There are vault toilets, picnic tables, and grills, but no drinking water or other facilities. Camping at the seven primitive sites costs $4, and the campground is open year-round. RVs and cars can fit onto the sites here.

There are also developed campgrounds and a number of primitive camping locations just outside the monument's boundaries. Backcountry camping is permitted in most areas of the monument with a free permit, available at the Interagency Office in Escalante and the BLM office in Kanab. (See "Information & Visitors Centers," above.)

Sports & Activities

This rugged national monument offers numerous opportunities for outdoor adventures, including **canyoneering** through narrow slot canyons, with the aid of ropes. You can get information on the best areas for canyoneering at the monument's visitor centers, but we cannot emphasize too strongly that this is not the place for beginners. To put it bluntly, people die here, and you don't want to be one of them.

We recommend that unless you are an expert at this specialized sport that you go with an expert. One of the best is Rick Green, owner of **Excursions of Escalante** ★★, 125 E. Main St. (P.O. Box 605), Escalante, UT 84726 (*©* **800/839-7567;** www. excursionsofescalante.com). Trips, which are available mid-March through mid-November, usually include four people with one guide, and all equipment is provided. In addition to canyoneering trips, the company offers day hiking and backpacking excursions, specialized tours, and 3-day canyoneering courses ($500–$600). Day trips include lunch. Day hiking trips cost $125 per person, canyoneering costs $145 to $165 per person, and a photo safari costs $170 per person. Overnight backpacking trips cost $250 to $275 per person per day, which includes practically everything you need, including food. Credit cards are not accepted; cash and checks are welcome. Excursions of Escalante also provides a flexible shuttle service; call for a quote.

HIKING, MOUNTAIN BIKING & HORSEBACK RIDING

Located about 15 miles northeast of Escalante via Utah 12, the **Calf Creek Recreation Area** has a campground (see "Camping," above), and a picnic area with fire grates and tables, trees, drinking water, and flush toilets. The best part of the recreation area, though, is the moderately strenuous 6-mile round-trip hike to **Lower Calf Creek Falls.** A sandy trail leads along Calf Creek, past beaver ponds and wetlands, to a beautiful waterfall, cascading 126 feet down a rock wall into a tree-shaded pool. You can pick up an interpretive brochure at the trail head. The day use fee is $2 per vehicle.

Although **Calf Creek Trail** is the monument's only officially marked and maintained trail, numerous unmarked cross-country routes are ideal for hiking, mountain biking (on existing dirt roads only), and horseback riding. We strongly recommend that hikers stop at the Interagency Office in Escalante or the BLM office in Kanab to get recommendations on hiking routes and to purchase topographic maps. (See "Information & Visitors Centers," above.) Hikers need to remember that this is wild country, and hiking can be hazardous. Rangers recommend carrying at least 1 gallon of water per person per day, and say that all water from streams should be treated before drinking. The potential for flooding is high, and hikers should check with the BLM before attempting to hike through the monument's narrow slot canyons. Other hazards include poisonous snakes, scorpions, and poison ivy. Slickrock, as the name suggests, is slippery, so hikers should wear sturdy hiking boots with traction soles.

Among the most popular and relatively easy-to-follow hiking routes is the footpath to **Escalante Natural Bridge.** The path repeatedly crosses the river, so be prepared to get wet up to your knees. The easy 2-mile (one-way) hike begins at a parking area off Utah 12 at the bridge that crosses the Escalante River near Calf Creek Recreation Area, 15 miles northeast of the town of Escalante. From the parking area, hike upstream to Escalante

These cliffs are bold escarpments, hundreds and thousands of feet in altitude—grand steps by which the region is terraced.
—Maj. John Wesley Powell, 1880

Natural Bridge, on the south side of the river. The stone bridge is 130 feet high and spans 100 feet.

Also starting at the Utah 12 bridge parking area is a hike downstream to **Phipps Wash.** Mostly moderate, this hike goes about 1.5 miles to the mouth of Phipps Wash, which enters the river from the west. You'll find Maverick Natural Bridge at the north side drainage of Phipps Wash, and climbing up the drainage on the south side leads to Phipps Arch.

Hiking the national monument's **slot canyons** is very popular, but we can't overemphasize the importance of checking on flood potentials before starting out. A sudden rainstorm, even one that's miles away, can cause a flash flood through a narrow canyon, trapping hikers.

One challenging and very strenuous slot-canyon hike is through **Peek-a-boo** and **Spooky canyons,** which are accessible from the Hole-in-the-Rock Scenic Backway. (See "Sightseeing & Four-Wheeling," below.) Stop at the Escalante Interagency Office (p. 114) for precise directions.

SIGHTSEEING & FOUR-WHEELING   Because it is one of America's least-developed sections of public land, Grand Staircase–Escalante National Monument offers a wonderful opportunity for exploration by the adventurous. Be aware, though, that the dirt roads inside the monument turn muddy—and impassable—when it rains.

One particularly popular road is the **Hole-in-the-Rock Scenic Backway,** which is partly in the national monument and partly in the adjacent Glen Canyon National Recreation Area. Like most roads in the monument, driving this route should be attempted in dry weather only. Starting about 5 miles northeast of Escalante off Utah 12, this clearly marked dirt road travels 57 miles (one-way) to the Hole-in-the-Rock, where Mormon settlers, in 1880, cut a passage through solid rock to get their wagons down a 1,200-foot cliff to the canyon floor and Colorado River below.

About 12 miles in, you'll encounter the sign for the **Devil's Rock Garden,** an area of classic red rock formations and arches,

8

NEARBY THINGS TO SEE & DO

Grand Staircase–Escalante National Monument

where you'll also find a picnic area (about a mile off the main road). The road continues across a plateau of typical desert terrain, ending at a spectacular scenic overlook of Lake Powell. The first 35 miles of the scenic byway are relatively easy (in dry weather) in a standard passenger car; it then gets a bit steeper and sandier, and the last 6 miles of the road require a high clearance four-wheel-drive vehicle. Allow about 6 hours round-trip, and make sure you have plenty of fuel and water.

Another recommended drive in the national monument is the **Cottonwood Canyon Road,** which runs from Kodachrome Basin State Park south to U.S. 89, along the monument's southern edge, a distance of about 46 miles. The road is sandy and narrow, but usually serviceable for passenger cars in dry weather. It mostly follows Cottonwood Wash, with good views of red rock formations and distant panoramas from hilltops. About 10 miles east of Kodachrome Basin State Park, you'll find a short side road to **Grosvenor Arch.** This magnificent stone arch, with an opening 99 feet wide, was named for National Geographic Society founder and editor Gilbert H. Grosvenor. Incidentally, a professional photographer friend of ours complained bitterly about the power lines that parallel the road, making scenic photography difficult. However, the BLM tells us that the road wouldn't exist at all if it weren't for those power lines.

WILDLIFE- & BIRD-WATCHING   This isolated and rugged terrain makes a good habitat for a number of species, including desert Bighorn sheep and mountain lions. More than 200 species of birds have been seen, including bald eagles, golden eagles, Swainson's hawks, and peregrine falcons. The best areas for seeing wildlife are along the Escalante and Paria rivers and Johnson Creek.

KODACHROME BASIN STATE PARK

About 22 miles E of the entrance to Bryce Canyon National Park

Kodachrome Basin lives up to its name—its wonderful scenery practically cries out to be photographed. Named for the classic Kodak color slide film by the National Geographic Society after an expedition there in 1948, the park is chock-full of tall stone chimneys and pink-and-white sandstone cliffs, all set among the contrasting greens of sagebrush and piñon and juniper trees. It also abuts and makes a good base for exploring Grand Staircase–Escalante National Monument (described earlier in the chapter).

Essentials

Because temperatures get a bit warm here in summer—the park is at 5,800 feet of elevation—the best times to visit, especially for hikers, are May, September, and October, when there are also fewer people.

GETTING THERE From Bryce Canyon National Park, go 3 miles north to the junction of Utah 63 and Utah 12, go east (right) on Utah 12 for about 12 miles to Cannonville, turn south onto the park's access road (there's a sign), and go about 9 miles to the park entrance.

INFORMATION, FEES & REGULATIONS Contact the **park office** at P.O. Box 180069, Cannonville, UT 84718-0069 (✆ **435/679-8562;** www.stateparks.utah.gov) for information. Day use costs $6 per vehicle. Dogs are permitted in the park and on trails, but must be kept on leashes no more than 6-feet long. The park office at the pay station at the entrance to the park can give you information.

CAMPING The park's attractive 27-site campground is set among stone chimneys and scattered piñon and juniper trees. It has flush toilets, showers, drinking water, picnic tables, barbecue grills, and an RV dump station. Four sites have full RV hookups. Basic campsites cost $16 per night, and sites with hookups cost $25 per night. Call ✆ **800/322-3770** or 801/322-3770 or visit www.reserveamerica.com for reservations ($8 reservation fee).

LODGING & SUPPLIES Located in the park along the park road (you can't miss it), **Kodachrome General Store** (✆ **435/ 679-8536;** www.redstonecabins.com) sells camping supplies, food items, and the like. This is also headquarters for **Redstone Cabins,** six modern cabins. Four have two double beds and two have one king, and all six have bathrooms with showers, refrigerators, microwaves, air-conditioning, private porches with tables and chairs, and outside charcoal barbecue grills. Cost per cabin per night for up to four people is $90 from mid-April to mid-October, $70 from mid-March to mid-April, and $50 the rest of the year.

Sports & Activities

HIKING Kodachrome Basin offers several hiking possibilities. Starting just south of the campground, the **Panorama Trail** is only moderately difficult. At first, it follows an old, relatively flat wagon route; then it climbs to offer views of the park's rock formations before reaching the well-named Panorama Point. Along the way are several possible side trips, including a short walk to the

Hat Shop, so named because the formations resemble broad-brimmed hats, and White Buffalo Loop, where you'll see a formation that looks like—guess what?—a white buffalo. On this hike, you can also hook up with Big Bear Geyser Trail, which is a bit more difficult, winding past Big Bear and Mama Bear before returning to Panorama Trail. Allow 2 to 3 hours for the Panorama Trail and an extra hour for Big Bear Geyser Trail.

Fans of arches will want to drive the dirt road to the trail head for the .5-mile round-trip hike to scenic Shakespeare Arch. This trail also provides views of a large chimney-rock formation.

HORSEBACK RIDING   To see Kodachrome Basin from the back of a horse contact Red Canyon Trail Rides (📞 800/892-7923; www.redcanyontrailrides.com). A 1-hour ride costs $30 and a 2-hour ride costs $50.

WILDLIFE-WATCHING   Jackrabbits and chukar partridges are probably the most commonly seen wildlife in the park. You'll also hear the piñon jay and might see an occasional coyote or rattlesnake.

CORAL PINK SAND DUNES STATE PARK

About 45 miles SE of Zion National Park

Long a favorite of dune-buggy enthusiasts, Coral Pink Sand Dunes has recently been attracting an increasing number of campers, hikers, photographers, and all-around nature lovers as well. While big boys—and some big girls—play with their expensive motorized toys, others hike; hunt for wildflowers, scorpions, and lizards; or just sit and wiggle their toes in the smooth, cool sand. The colors are especially rich at sunrise and sunset. Early-morning visitors will find the tracks of yesterday's dune buggies gone, replaced by the tracks of lizards, kangaroo rats, snakes, and the rest of the park's animal kingdom, who venture out in the coolness of night, once all the people have departed.

Essentials

At about 6,000 feet of elevation, the park gets warm in summer, with temperatures easily reaching the mid-90s Fahrenheit (in the neighborhood of 35°C). Winters are usually relatively mild, although snow and bitterly cold temperatures are not unheard of. Our choice for a visit is May, June, September, or October, when it's delightfully cool at night but warm enough during the day to enjoy burying your toes in the cooling sand. There are also fewer people there at those times.

GETTING THERE From Zion National Park, take Utah 9 east to U.S. 89, turn right (south) and continue to the park entrance road. From downtown Kanab, go about 8 miles north on U.S. 89, then southwest (left) on Hancock Road for about 12 miles to get to the park.

INFORMATION & VISITOR CENTER For copies of the park brochure and off-highway-vehicle regulations, contact the **park office** at P.O. Box 95, Kanab, UT 84741-0095 (℃ **435/648-2800**). Information is also available online at www.stateparks. utah.gov. At the **park entry station,** which also serves as a visitor center, you'll see a small display area with sand from around the world, fossils from the area, and live scorpions, lizards, and tadpoles. This is the place to find out about ranger programs.

FEES & REGULATIONS The day-use fee is $6 per vehicle. The standard state park regulations apply, with the addition of a few extra rules due to the park's popularity with off-road-vehicle users. Quiet hours last from 10pm to 9am. The dunes are open to motor vehicles between 9am and 10pm and to hikers at any time. Vehicles going onto the dunes must have safety flags, available at the entry station; while on the dunes, they must stay at least 10 feet from vegetation and at least 100 feet from hikers. Dogs are permitted on the dunes but must be leashed.

CAMPING The spacious and mostly shady 22-site campground, open year-round, offers hot showers, modern restrooms, and an RV dump station, but no hookups. Camping costs $16 and sites can be reserved (℃ **800/322-3770** or 801/322-3770; www.reserve america.com), with an $8 nonrefundable reservation fee.

RANGER PROGRAMS Regularly scheduled ranger talks explain the geology, plants, and animals of the dunes. For a real thrill, take a guided evening **Scorpion Walk** ★★, using a black light to find the luminescent scorpions that make the park their home. You'll definitely want to wear shoes for this activity! Call to find out if there's a Scorpion Walk scheduled during your visit.

Sports & Activities

HIKING The best time for hiking the dunes is early morning, for several reasons: It's cooler, the lighting at and just after sunrise produces beautiful shadows and colors, and there are no noisy dune buggies until after 9am. Sunset is also very pretty, but you'll be sharing the dunes with off-road vehicles. Keep in mind that hiking through fine sand can be very tiring, especially for those who go barefoot. A self-guided .5-mile loop nature trail has numbered signs through some of the dunes; allow a half-hour.

Several other hikes of various lengths are possible within and just outside the park, but because there are few signs—and because landmarks change with the shifting sands—it's best to check with park rangers before setting out. Those spending more than a few hours in the dunes will discover that even their own tracks disappear in the wind, leaving few clues to the route back to park headquarters.

OFF-ROADING   This giant sandbox offers plenty of space for **off-road-vehicle enthusiasts.** Because the sand here is quite fine, extra-wide flotation tires are needed, and lightweight dune buggies are usually the vehicle of choice. If exploring the park itself isn't enough for you, adjacent to the park, on Bureau of Land Management property, you'll find hundreds of miles of trails and roads for off-highway vehicles.

ESCALANTE PETRIFIED FOREST STATE PARK

44 miles E of Bryce Canyon National Park

Large chunks of colorful petrified wood decorate this unique park, which offers hiking, fishing, boating, camping, and panoramic vistas of the surrounding countryside. There's wildlife to watch, trails to hike, and a 30-acre reservoir for boating, fishing, and somewhat chilly swimming.

Essentials

The park is open year-round, but spring through fall is the best time to visit. Hikers should be prepared for hot summer temperatures and carry plenty of water.

GETTING THERE   The park is 44 miles from Bryce Canyon. It's located about 2 miles southwest of Escalante, on Utah 12, at Wide Hollow Road.

INFORMATION & VISITOR CENTER   Contact **Escalante Petrified Forest State Park,** 710 N. Reservoir Rd., Escalante, UT 84776 (*(C)* **435/826-4466;** www.stateparks.utah.gov). The **visitor center,** open daily, has displays of petrified wood, fossils, and dinosaur bones more than 100 million years old, plus an exhibit explaining how petrified wood is formed.

FEES & REGULATIONS   Entry costs $6 per vehicle, which includes boat launching. As at most parks, regulations are generally based on common sense and courtesy: Don't damage anything, drive slowly on park roads, and observe quiet hours between 10pm

ROCK OR WOOD—WHAT IS THIS STUFF?

It looks like a weathered, multicolored tree limb, shining and sparkling in the light—but it's heavy, hard, and solid as a rock. Just what is this stuff? It's **petrified wood.** Back in the old days—some 135 to 155 million years ago—southern Utah was not at all the way it is today. It was closer to the equator than it is now, which made it a wet, hot land, with lots of ferns, palm trees, and conifers that provided lunch for the neighborhood dinosaurs. Occasionally, floods would uproot trees, dumping them in flood plains and along sandbars, and then burying them with mud and silt. If this happened quickly, the layers of mud and silt would cut off the oxygen supply, halting the process of decomposition—effectively preserving the tree trunks intact. Later, volcanic ash covered the area, and groundwater rich in silicon dioxide and other chemicals and minerals made its way down to the ancient trees. With the silicon dioxide acting as a glue, the cells of the wood mineralized. Other waterborne minerals produced the colors: Iron painted the tree trunks in reds, browns, and yellows; manganese produced purples and blues. Sometime afterward, uplifts from within the earth, along with various forms of erosion, brought the now-petrified wood to the surface in such places as Escalante Petrified Forest State Park and the Grand Staircase–Escalante National Monument, breaking it into the shapes we see today—a mere hundred million years or so after the trees were first uprooted.

and 7am. In addition, you're asked to resist the temptation to carry off samples of petrified wood. Pets are welcome, even on trails, but must be on leashes no more than 6 feet long.

CAMPING The 22-unit RV and tent **campground,** within easy walking distance of the park's hiking trails and reservoir, is open year-round. Facilities include hot showers, modern restrooms, and drinking water. There are four sites with water and electric RV hookups. Camping costs $16 per night, $20 with hookups. Reservations are available at ✆ **800/322-3770** or 801/322-3770 (www.reserveamerica.com); an $8 nonrefundable fee will be charged.

Sports & Activities

FISHING & BOATING Wide Hollow Reservoir, located partially inside the park, has a boat ramp (sorry, no rentals are available) and is a popular fishing hole for rainbow trout and blue-gill, plus ice-fishing in winter.

HIKING The 1-mile loop **Petrified Forest Trail ★** is a moderately strenuous hike among colorful rocks, through a forest of stunted juniper and piñon pine, past a painted desert, to a field of colorful petrified wood. The hike also offers panoramic vistas of the town of Escalante and surrounding stair-step plateaus. A free brochure is available at the visitor center. Allow about 45 minutes. An optional .75-mile loop off the main trail—called **Trail of Sleeping Rainbows**—leads through a large amount of petrified wood, but is considerably steeper than the main trail.

WILDLIFE-WATCHING This is one of the best spots in the region to see wildlife. The reservoir is home to ducks, geese, and coots. Chukar partridges wander throughout the park, and you're also likely to see eagles, hawks, lizards, ground squirrels, and both cottontails and jackrabbits. Binoculars are helpful.

SNOW CANYON STATE PARK

11 miles NW of St. George; about 60 miles W of Zion National Park

Among Utah's most scenic state parks, **Snow Canyon ★★** offers an abundance of opportunities for photography and hiking. The park is surrounded by rock cliffs and walls of Navajo sandstone in every shade of red imaginable, layered with white and black from ancient lava flows. Hike the trails and discover shifting sand dunes, mysterious lava caves, colorful desert plants, and a variety of rock formations. You'll also encounter an attractive cactus garden and several ancient petroglyphs. (Ask park rangers for directions.) By the way, don't come here looking for snow—the canyon was named for pioneers Lorenzo and Erastus Snow, who reportedly discovered it.

Essentials

Because the summers here are hot—well over 100°F (38°C)—the best time to visit is any other time. Winters are mild, but nights can be chilly. Spring and fall are usually perfect weather-wise, and are therefore the busiest. Elevation is 3,200 feet.

GETTING THERE From Zion National Park, follow Utah 9 to exit 16 off I-15, head south to St. George (exit 8), and take Utah 18 northwest to the park's entrance road.

INFORMATION, FEES & REGULATIONS For a copy of the park's brochure and other information, contact **Snow Canyon State Park,** 1002 Snow Canyon Dr., Ivins, UT 84738-6194 (✆ **435/628-2255**), or stop at the visitor center, open daily, when you arrive. Information is also available online at www.stateparks. utah.gov. The day-use fee is $6 per vehicle. As in most Utah state parks, dogs are welcome, including on trails, but must be leashed.

CAMPING   The park's 31-site campground ★★ is one of the best in the Utah state park system. One section has rather closely spaced sites with electric and water hookups; those not needing hookups can set up camp in delightful little side canyons, surrounded by colorful red rocks and Utah juniper. The views are spectacular no matter where you choose to set up. Facilities include hot showers, modern restrooms, and an RV dump station. Campsites with hook-ups cost $20, while those without are $16. Reservations (with an $8 nonrefundable reservation fee) are recommended February through May and September through November; call ✆ **800/322-3770** or 801/322-3770, or visit www.reserveamerica.com.

Sports & Activities

HIKING   The best way to see Snow Canyon is on foot, and the park has 16 miles of trails. Several short trails make for easy full- or half-day hikes. The **Hidden Piñon Trail** is a 1.5-mile round-trip self-guided nature trail that wanders among lava rocks, through several canyons, and onto rocky flatlands, offering panoramic views of the surrounding mountains. The trail begins across the highway from the campground; you can pick up a brochure at the park office/ entrance station. The walk is fairly easy, but allow at least an hour. Keep an eye out for Mormon tea, cliffrose, prickly pear cactus, and banana yucca.

The easy 2-mile round-trip **Johnson Canyon Trail,** open in winter only, begins just south of the campground, passes by the popular rock-climbing wall (described below), some low sand dunes, and then a small canyon with a view of Johnson Arch (named after pioneer wife Maude Johnson) high above.

Also popular is the **Lava Flow Overlook Trail,** a 2-mile round-trip that starts about a quarter-mile north of Snow Canyon Over-look, on Utah 18. The trail offers a variety of panoramic views, including West Canyon Overlook, with a breathtaking view into West Canyon.

Several longer and steeper trails lead to spectacular views of the canyons and distant vistas; check with park rangers for details.

MOUNTAIN BIKING   Although bicycling is not allowed on most park trails, it is permitted on the 6-mile round-trip Whiptail Trail, a paved trail along the bottom of the canyon. You can also bike West Canyon Road, a 7-mile round-trip route just west of the park (ask rangers for directions).

ROCK CLIMBING   Very popular with technical rock climbers, Snow Canyon has more than 170 designated routes, including the tall wall of rock on the east side of the road just south of the campground. Get a map of the climbing areas and route information from the park office.

WILDLIFE-WATCHING   You're likely to see cottontail rabbits, ground squirrels, and songbirds; luckier visitors may also spot desert mule deer, bobcats, coyote, kit foxes, eagles, and owls. Although it's unlikely, you may see a desert tortoise (a federally listed threatened species) or Gila monster. Snow Canyon is also home to some rattlesnakes, which you'll want to avoid.

A NATURE GUIDE TO ZION & BRYCE CANYON NATIONAL PARKS

9

M agnificently diverse, Zion and Bryce Canyon national parks contain burning deserts, lush woodlands with shimmering ponds, barren, windswept ledges of solid rock, and deep forests of pine and fir. These habitats, with their variety of terrain and climates, support a wide array of plants and animals whose diversity is primarily a result of the wide range of elevations and the differing availability of water. Zion, ranging from 3,666 to 8,726 feet above sea level, has a larger variety of plants and animals than cooler and higher Bryce Canyon, with elevations from 6,620 to 9,115 feet.

ZION & BRYCE CANYON NATIONAL PARKS TODAY

While much of southern Utah is barren and sometimes drab desert, Zion and Bryce Canyon are most certainly much more. (That is, of course, why they were designated national parks in the first place.) Those with the time and inclination to explore these parks will discover hundreds of microclimates—little worlds of their own that create unique habitats that often seem out of place in this generally arid country.

In Zion, you can see several of these microclimates along the **Riverside Walk**—there's a desert swamp where you might spot a leopard frog or two, and lush, hanging gardens on the walls as you enter the **Narrows.** You'll also find hanging gardens at **Zion's Weeping Rock,** where there is a good example of *spring lines,* which occur when water seeping through a porous rock is diverted to the surface by a layer of much harder rock.

At Bryce Canyon, you'll discover a moist world in the aptly named **Mossy Cave,** which is fed by a natural spring. Walking down the **Queen's Garden Trail,** you'll notice that the vegetation on the north-facing slopes and in the narrow gullies—Douglas fir and ponderosa pines—is far different than the piñon and juniper in the sunnier areas. And there is a much cooler and wetter climate at the higher elevations in the southern section of the park—such as along the **Bristlecone Loop** and **Riggs Spring Loop** trails.

Bryce Canyon at first seems easy to understand—it's the hoodoos, of course—but look a bit closer and you'll soon realize that in addition to its delightful rock formations, Bryce Canyon has serene woodlands of pine, where deer graze in open meadows, and dense forests of spruce and fir, where you'll find the world's oldest living organisms—bristlecone pines. Of course, there are also the lowlands, below the rim. This is definitely a desert, yet anything but drab, with its colorful and whimsical hoodoos.

Zion has a more complicated environment. There are stupendous rock formations—even a few hoodoos—but Zion also has the unique Narrows, a canyon carved by the Virgin River, which is home to fascinating microclimates and habitats that support plants and animals not seen elsewhere in the park. These include the rare Zion snail, found nowhere else in the world. In some ways, Zion has even more diverse geographic features than Bryce Canyon—everything from delightful little pools surrounded by delicate ferns and wildflowers to rocky, windswept ridges, where only the most determined and rugged plants and animals can survive.

The best way to explore these parks and get to know them intimately is to get away from the viewpoints and hit the trails, leaving behind the throngs, who seem to be glued to the officially designated scenic lookouts. Remember, though, that southern Utah is hot in the summer, and these parks—particularly lower-elevation Zion and some of the trails below the rim at Bryce Canyon—can be scorching desert, so be prepared with plenty of drinking water and sun block.

On the other hand, it is also possible to get a close-up view of nature without exerting a lot of effort. Plants and rocks are everywhere, and a variety of animals can be seen throughout both parks. To see wildlife, simply go to a quiet place—even a park campground early in the morning—and wait. Sit at the edge of a meadow or take a slow walk down almost any park path or trail—the key here is to get away from people, and especially the noise they make, and to take the time to watch, wait, and listen. Nature surrounds you at both Bryce Canyon and Zion national parks, but it doesn't necessarily advertise itself; with just a bit of patience, it can be coaxed out of hiding.

THE LANDSCAPE

There are many reasons to visit Zion and Bryce Canyon national parks, but what you'll find in almost all sections of both parks—and probably what you came to experience—are their intricately sculpted and often beautifully colored rocks, from majestic, towering formations like the Great White Throne at Zion, to the delicately carved and whimsical hoodoos at Bryce Canyon. For these we can thank the geologic processes of uplifting and erosion.

The parks are located on the northwestern edge of the Colorado Plateau, a 130,000-square-mile region that covers the Four Corners area and encompasses about half of Utah, most of northern Arizona (including the Grand Canyon), much of western Colorado, and the northwest corner of New Mexico. Named for the Colorado River, which is responsible for carving many of the area's scenic canyons, the Colorado Plateau began as the result of uplifting 10 to 15 million years ago. Large, flat beds of sedimentary rock created from different minerals—or combinations of minerals—resulted in layers of varying densities. Forces within the earth pushed some of these sections of sediment up out of the earth. This uplift is especially noticeable in places such as Zion and Bryce Canyon. Here, uplifts along geologic fault lines created high plateaus with large chunks of rock, where you can see the stripes of the different layers of rock.

When wind and water began their inevitable erosion, layers of softer rock, such as sandstone and limestone, wore down faster than the harder layers of mudstone and shale. This created intricate and sometimes bizarre shapes. For example, the formation called **Thor's Hammer,** in Bryce Canyon, owes its hammerlike shape to a variety of rock densities—the hammer section on top is harder and more resistant to erosion than the softer handle section

HOW NATURE paints THE PARKS

The shapes are fantastic—towering monoliths, massive mesas of stone, delicate spires, intricately carved sculptures, and squat little toadstools—but what first catches our eyes are the delightful colors. What seems like an infinite variety of hues elevates these parks from geologic wonders to exquisite works of art. But where do the colors come from? What dynamic forces have meticulously painted these stone sculptures so perfectly?

The answer, simply and unpoetically put, is rust. Most of the rocks at Zion and Bryce Canyon are colored by iron, or hematite (iron oxide), either contained in the original stone or carried into the rocks by groundwater. Although iron most often creates red and pink hues, frequently seen in Zion's towering sandstone faces and Bryce Canyon's spectacular amphitheaters, it can also result in blacks, browns, yellows, and even greens. Sometimes the iron seeps into the rock, coloring it through, but it can also stain just the surface, often in vertical streaks.

Rocks are also colored by the bacteria that live on their surfaces. These bacteria ingest dust and expel iron, manganese, and other minerals, which then stick to the rock, producing a shiny black, brown, or reddish surface called desert varnish. Last, but certainly not least, is the work of water, which deposits salt as it evaporates, creating white streaks.

below. Eventually, the handle will crumble and the hammerhead will come crashing to the ground. Erosion, as well as the shifting and breaking of rock, carved the sculptures of Zion and Bryce Canyon. The process almost always involves water and gravity, although wind and temperature, primarily freezing and thawing, play an important role as well.

Although there are also hoodoos similar to Thor's Hammer in Zion—mostly on the park's east side—many of Zion's rock formations appear more massive and rugged. But here, too, the rocks have been carved by the forces of nature, primarily water, as can be seen clearly when looking up from the bottom of the **Narrows.** This incredibly slim canyon—1,000 feet high but less than 30 feet wide in some places—was meticulously carved through Navajo sandstone by the North Fork of the Virgin River.

The most important of Zion's nine rock layers—at least in the creation of those imposing rock formations—is **Navajo sandstone,** which is the thickest rock layer in the park, at up to 2,200 feet. The sandstone layer was created some 200 million years ago, during the Jurassic period, when most of North America was hot and dry. Movements in the earth's crust enabled a shallow sea to form over windblown sand dunes. Then minerals, including lime from the shells of sea creatures, eventually glued sand particles together to form sandstone. Later, crust movements caused the land to uplift, draining away the sea, but leaving rivers that gradually carved the relatively soft sandstone into the spectacular shapes we see today.

By comparison, Bryce Canyon is a mere babe. Its rocks were formed some 64 million years ago, created from sediments that were left behind when ancient lakes and rivers dried up. As at neighboring Zion, these rock layers were then uplifted and exposed to the ravages of nature. Much of Bryce Canyon's rock is **limestone,** relatively soft and crumbly, which was easily eroded into the park's numerous intricate hoodoos. The processes that created the rock formation in both parks continue today. Even to the naked eye, it's possible to see the changes that weathering has produced on Bryce Canyon's famous **Queen Victoria** hoodoo over the past 25 years.

THE FLORA

Great variations in elevation and the availability of water have resulted in numerous microclimates throughout these two parks. In one section, you can see desert grasses, sagebrush, and a few cacti; while in another, not far away, there might be deep green woods where maidenhair ferns and cottonwood trees thrive. Zion National Park boasts over 900 species of plants—considered the richest diversity of plants in Utah—while at Bryce Canyon the number is a bit over 400. In the lower elevations, particularly in the hot, dry desert areas of Zion, you'll find cactus, mesquite, and yucca. As elevation increases, juniper and piñon are added, and eventually, in the high mountains of Bryce Canyon, you encounter a deep forest of fir and spruce, with stands of quaking aspen that turn a magnificent bright yellow each fall.

While exploring Zion, be sure to watch for spring lines and their lush hanging gardens, which you'll see clinging to the sides of cliffs. Because sandstone is porous, water can percolate down through it until a harder layer of rock stops it. At that point, the water simply changes direction, moving horizontally to the rock face, where it oozes out, forming the spring line that provides life-giving nutrients to whatever seeds the wind delivers.

Trees

ASPEN   The most widely distributed tree in North America, growing from Alaska to southern Arizona, **quaking aspen** are

Quaking Aspen   *Bristlecone Pine*

found in Utah, above 7,500 feet of elevation, mostly above the rim and in the mountains at the southern end of Bryce Canyon, and along the cliffs and plateaus at Zion. Named "quaking" for the trembling movement of the leaves at the slightest wind, aspens have white bark and almost heart-shaped green leaves that urn a striking yellow or gold in the fall. Deer and elk eat the twigs and leaves, and rabbits and other small mammals eat the leaves, buds, and bark.

BRISTLECONE PINE   The oldest known trees—some have lived more than 4,600 years—bristlecones that are more than 1,600 years old can be found at Bryce Canyon, usually along exposed, rocky slopes above 7,500 feet of elevation. Bristlecones have very short dark-green needles, which grow all around each branch and are often tightly packed, and dark-brown, cylindrical cones. The trees commonly have a gnarled, weathered appearance, due at least in part to their age and choice of environment.

Fremont Cottonwood

COTTONWOOD   A member of the willow family, cottonwoods like lots of water and are usually found along streams or other permanent water sources. The **narrowleaf cottonwood,** found along water in Bryce Canyon, has skinny, green willowlike leaves that turn dull yellow in the fall. The **Fremont cottonwood,** found

Douglas Fir   *Juniper*

in almost all moist areas of Zion, has large, triangular-shaped, shiny yellow-green leaves that turn bright yellow in the fall.

DOUGLAS FIR   This large evergreen—some can grow as tall as 200 feet—has medium-size, blue-green needles and fairly large cones. Birds and various mammals eat the seeds, while deer eat the foliage. The Douglas fir is found at most elevations in the canyons and on the plateaus at Zion National Park. (There are good stands on the Kolob Terrace.) At Bryce Canyon, you'll find Douglas fir primarily above 7,500 feet of elevation, especially in the southern part of the park.

JUNIPER   Two types of juniper—**Rocky Mountain** and **Utah**—grow in the parks, most often in canyons and on rocky slopes. Utah juniper are usually seen at the lower and drier elevations—below the rim at Bryce Canyon—while Rocky Mountain juniper will grow throughout the parks up to 8,500 feet of elevation. The Utah juniper has a short trunk and low spreading branches, with closely spaced yellow-green needles; the Rocky Mountain juniper is often taller, sometimes reaching 50 feet, with slender branches and short, gray-green needles. Both have berrylike cones that are a popular food for birds and other wildlife. The Utah juniper's "berries" are a dull blue, while the "berries" of the Rocky Mountain juniper are bright blue with a white coating.

PIÑON PINE   Common throughout the southern Rocky Mountains, between 5,000 and 7,000 feet of elevation, piñon are found at both parks, although mostly below the rim at Bryce Canyon. They are usually fairly small and somewhat gnarled, with rough

Piñon Pine

bark and light green needles up to 1½ inches long that usually grow in bundles of two. The small, egg-shaped cones produce edible seeds, often called nuts, which are a popular food for both humans and wildlife. The piñon jay takes its name from the tree and its tasty seeds.

Ponderosa Pine

PONDEROSA PINE This large, impressive tree, which is found in both parks, is easily recognized by its long needles—up to 10 inches—that usually grow in bundles of three. Adult trees have orange-tinted bark that has a fragrance similar to vanilla, and large reddish-brown cones that are round or egg-shaped. At Zion, look for the ponderosa pine along cliffs and high plateaus; it is found at Bryce Canyon on sunny slopes above and along the rim, in the campgrounds, and around the lodge.

Shrubs & Ferns

MAIDENHAIR FERN A surprise in southern Utah's generally arid terrain, this moisture-loving fern, known for its delicate, lacy fronds and thin black stems, thrives in select areas of Zion National Park, near sources of water such as the Emerald Pools, and in hanging gardens, including those at Weeping Rock.

SAGEBRUSH Covering much of the American West, various types of sagebrush are found throughout Zion and Bryce Canyon. A shrub that normally grows in alkaline soil in arid areas, it can reach several feet tall, if it gets sufficient water. A common food for deer and other animals, sagebrush has a fresh, pungent scent—strongest when it's wet—that is similar to the spice sage. It has tiny, gray-green leaves and sprouts small, white flowers in the fall. Three varieties grow at Bryce Canyon: **big, black,** and **fringed;** while **big** and **old man** grow at Zion.

YUCCA Not a cactus as many think, but a shrub, yuccas grow in dry, rocky areas of both parks. One of the prettiest plants in the Southwest—absolutely stunning when it's in bloom—the yucca was extremely important to early American Indians, who made baskets and sandals from its strong leaves, ate its fruits and flowers, and turned its roots into a shampoo. The plant has long, extremely tough green leaves with sharp spines on their tips that can be quite painful to the touch. In the spring or early summer, the yucca produces a tall stalk of large, white flowers. You'll find the **narrow-leaf yucca** at Bryce Canyon, and the **Datil** (broad-leaf) and **Utah** varieties at Zion.

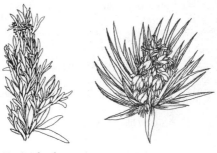

Big Sagebrush   *Yucca*

Flowering Plants

CLARET CUP CACTUS One of 14 varieties of cactus found in the desert areas of Zion National Park, the claret cup boasts one of the park's most beautiful flowers and usually produces its brilliant red blooms in the spring, sometimes as early as March. The cactus stem (the body) is gray-green, cylindrical, 3 to 4 inches across, and covered with long, sharp, curved spines. As plants

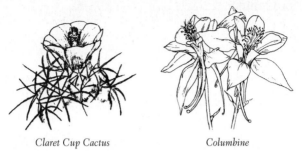

Claret Cup Cactus   Columbine

mature, numerous stems may grow, and they are stunning when covered with flowers.

COLUMBINE   A member of the buttercup family, columbine comes in a variety of shapes and colors. Flowers have five petals, but the overall appearance can vary quite a bit. Columbine usually prefers shady, moist areas, such as Zion's hanging gardens, but will also grow in rocky canyons and open meadows. Species at Zion are the **golden columbine** (with a beautiful yellow flower) and the **western columbine** (with red and yellow flowers). In Bryce Canyon, you'll find **blue columbine** (the Colorado state flower) in meadows above 7,500 feet and in the high forest at the southern end of the park. Blooming season is late spring and early summer at Zion, and from mid- to late summer at Bryce Canyon.

LARKSPUR   Another member of the buttercup family, the larkspur is represented by several families in the drier areas of both parks, blooming in summer. Flowers are small—about 1 inch across—and are blue, violet, or white.

PRICKLY PEAR CACTUS   One of the easiest types of cactus to identify, as well as one of the most common, prickly pears have flattened paddle-shaped pads covered with spines. You'll find them throughout the drier areas of both parks, up to about 8,500 feet. Prickly pear usually bloom in late spring or early summer at Zion, a little later in Bryce Canyon, and the cacti produce pretty flowers, about 2 to 3 inches across. Flowers are mostly

Larkspur

bright yellow, but sometimes pink or magenta. The plains and Engelmann prickly pear you see at Zion are similar to the types usually encountered throughout the Southwest, with dull green pads and rigid spines an inch or so long. A bit unusual is the grizzly bear prickly pear that grows at Bryce Canyon. Although its pads are similar to other prickly pears, you can hardly see them because of what looks like long hair but are actually spines, which are flexible, white, and sometimes up to a foot long.

Prickly Pear Cactus

SACRED DATURA   Dubbed the "Zion Lily" because of its abundance in the park, the sacred datura has large, funnel-shaped white flowers that open in the cool of night and are often closed by noon the next day. You'll see them frequently along roadsides and other areas where the soil has been disturbed, generally in dry, sandy soil below 7,000 feet of elevation. Also called the Southwestern thorn apple, the sacred datura's flowers are 5 to 8 inches long and just as wide—the largest blossoms of any plant in southern Utah—and bloom from early spring to fall. Because it blossoms at night, it is also sometimes called the moon lily. **Warning:** The sacred datura is highly poisonous, and if any part of the plant is ingested, it is likely to cause hallucinations, convulsions, and quite possibly death.

SEGO LILY   Found in the drier areas below the rim in Bryce Canyon and in the canyons, cliffs, and plateaus of Zion, the sego lily has delicate white flowers, each about 1 to 2 inches wide. Flowers appear in late spring or early summer, and each is bell

Sacred Datura

Sego Lily

shaped, with three petals. The sego lily is the Utah state flower, and the state's early Mormon settlers ate the plant's bulbs when food was scarce.

THE FAUNA

Just as with these parks' plant life, elevation and availability of water determine what animals you'll see in any particular area. Zion, again, has the most diversity, with 78 species of mammals, 291 species of birds, and 44 species of reptiles and amphibians. Bryce Canyon also has plenty of wildlife to spot, with 59 species of mammals, 175 species of birds, and about 15 species of reptiles and amphibians. Most of the animals in the lower elevations are those of the desert—small creatures such as lizards and snakes, kangaroo rats, rabbits, and squirrels. As the elevation increases, watch for prairie dogs, beavers, Bighorn sheep, and mule deer. In the high forests of Bryce Canyon, keep an eye out for elk, pronghorn, and, possibly, black bear.

Mammals

BIGHORN SHEEP Named for the large, curving horns that the rams possess, **desert Bighorn sheep** are brown or light tan, with prominent white splotches on their rumps, faces, and legs. They inhabit isolated and harsh desert environments—what appear to be the most inhospitable areas. Your best bet for seeing Bighorn sheep is in the steep, rocky areas on the east side of Zion National Park. They eat a variety of grasses and shrubs—practically whatever is available—and can go without water for more than 5 days.

BLACK BEARS Although often black in the eastern United States, black bears in the West are usually brown or even tan. The males are big, up to about 6 feet tall and weighing over 500 pounds; the females are much smaller. Bears like wooded areas, usually below 7,000 feet of elevation, and there are occasional

Bighorn
Sheep

Black Bear

THE return OF THE BIGHORN SHEEP

Prior to the 20th century, there were reports of significant numbers of desert Bighorns in the area now known as Zion National Park. However, the population gradually declined. This decline was due primarily to development of the land by settlers, who blocked access to water, planted crops, and brought in livestock that not only competed with the Bighorns for grazing land but also introduced diseases. Another problem for the Bighorns came with construction of the Zion–Mt. Carmel Highway and Tunnel in the 1920s, which effectively chopped the Bighorn's range in half. Park officials estimated that by the 1930s, there were about 25 Bighorns in the park, and, by the late 1950s, there were none left.

Reintroduction efforts began in the mid-1960s, although it was not until 1973 that a dozen desert Bighorns were captured in southern Nevada and brought to the park, where they were kept in an 80-acre enclosure. By 1976, there were 22 Bighorns, still trapped in the enclosure, and park service wildlife biologists decided to release 13, moving them by helicopter to an isolated canyon in the southeastern corner of the park. Unfortunately, by the next year only 4 of the 13 had survived in the wild (many were killed by mountain lions), and this part of the reintroduction effort was considered a failure. By 1978, the population of the Bighorns that remained in the enclosure had increased to 20, and they were released into the park. Although nine died over the course of the next year, this release was considered a success.

Today there are at least 65 Bighorns at Zion and sightings are fairly common. It appears that the herd is making a successful comeback, both in terms of reproduction and range expansion. Park officials believe the park could support at least twice as many desert Bighorns, but for the time being, there are no plans to introduce more from other areas, in part because of the fear that new animals would bring in new diseases.

sightings in both parks. However, rather than actually seeing a bear in the flesh (or the fur), it's more likely that you'll see signs of the bear's presence, such as scat (bear droppings), decayed stumps or logs that have been torn apart for the grubs they contained, or tooth and claw marks on trees. Interestingly, bear footprints look similar to those made by humans, with the addition of a small round mark above each toe produced by the bear's claws.

Chipmunk

CHIPMUNKS Of the 22 species of chipmunks in North America, 21 can be found in the western United States. It is often difficult to tell one chipmunk species from another (at least for humans), but it's usually fairly easy to distinguish chipmunks from their cousins the squirrels, because chipmunks have black-and-white facial stripes and squirrels do not. The Uinta, least, and cliff species of chipmunks are found at both Bryce Canyon and Zion. The **cliff chipmunk,** which is often seen in rocky areas near cliffs, is usually the biggest of the three, sometimes reaching more than 10 inches long. The **Uinta** is usually seen scurrying about in pine and fir forests, such as those in both parks' campgrounds, while the **least chipmunks** are at home in open areas of desert terrain, such as the beginning sections of the Under the Rim Trail, at Bryce Canyon. All three have brown and gray fur, and black-and-white stripes on their backs (although the cliff chipmunks' stripes may be less distinct than the others), in addition to facial stripes.

Coyote

Elk

COYOTES Coyotes are survivors, and they are increasing in population throughout the United States. They are seen—or more often heard—throughout both Zion and Bryce Canyon, where they hunt rabbits, rodents, and other small animals. Tan or yellow-gray, with bushy tails, coyotes look much like domestic dogs and usually weigh 30 to 40 pounds. They can run at over 25 mph, reaching 40 mph for short periods. One way to easily distinguish between a dog and a coyote is that coyotes run with their tails down, while domestic dogs run with their tails up. Coyote choruses are often heard at night, consisting of a series of sharp yelps, barks, and howls.

ELK Although not believed to be full-time residents of either park, **Rocky Mountain elk** are known to frequent the area and are sometimes spotted in or near the parks at the higher elevations, particularly in the fir and spruce forest at the southern end of Bryce Canyon

National Park, and the Kolob Plateau in the northern part of Zion. Known for the buck's large racks of antlers, Rocky Mountain elk can reach weights of more than 1,000 pounds. Their coloring is usually brown or tan, with hints of yellow on their rumps and tails.

MOUNTAIN LIONS These large cats, usually solid tan or beige, are also known as panthers, cougars, and pumas. They are occasionally seen in both Bryce Canyon and Zion national parks. However, there have been more sightings in Zion than in Bryce Canyon in recent years, and it is believed

Mountain Lion

that there are quite a few in the backcountry areas of Kolob Canyon. Because they avoid humans, your best chance of seeing one is in a remote area or along a quiet roadway late at night. At Bryce Canyon, you are most likely to see a mountain lion in the southern part of the park, in the backcountry along the Riggs Spring Loop Trail. Skilled hunters, mountain lions prefer to catch deer, and a single mountain lion can kill and consume a mule deer a week, if deer are plentiful. They also hunt coyotes, beavers, small mammals, and birds. Mountain lions will usually stash the leftovers from their kills, covering them with brush, sticks, and leaves, for later consumption.

MULE DEER The most commonly seen large animals at both parks, mule deer are often spotted near the campgrounds at Zion and along the Bryce Canyon scenic drive, especially in meadows along the edge of the forest. Considered medium-size as deer go, mule deer are usually reddish brown in summer and gray during the winter, with patches of white on their rumps and throats year-round. Their most

Mule Deer

distinguishing characteristic—which has given them their name— is their pair of huge, mulelike ears. Bucks can weigh up to 450 pounds, while doe usually weigh about one-third of that.

PRAIRIE DOG These cute little critters are not dogs at all, but members of the squirrel family, making them rodents. The species at Bryce Canyon—the **Utah prairie dog**—is listed as a threatened species, which both amuses and annoys southern Utah ranchers, who consider it a pest. Utah prairie dogs are about a foot long, reddish-tan, and have small ears. Active during the day, prairie dogs live in park meadows in busy communities comprised of burrows, with mounds of dirt at each entrance. These colonies are strategically

Prairie Dog

located in areas that have enough grass and other plants to sustain them, but with vegetation that is sparse and low enough for them to be able to spot predators with enough time to dart into their burrows. Prairie dogs seem to delight in alternately running about and standing at attention, and their antics are popular with park visitors.

Warning: The bacteria that cause bubonic plague has been found on fleas in prairie dog colonies in Bryce Canyon, so you should avoid getting too close. Plus, they bite.

PRONGHORN Commonly seen in open fields in the vicinity of Bryce Canyon National Park—both within and outside the park—

Pronghorn

pronghorns were reintroduced into the area after practically being eliminated in the late 1800s and early 1900s. Sometimes called the American antelope, pronghorns are usually reddish-tan, with white on their rump, chest, stomach, lower parts of their face, and inner legs. The fastest animals in the Western Hemisphere—and the second fastest in the world behind the African cheetah—pronghorns can reach speeds of 70 mph, and their speed, combined with excellent eyesight, enable them to escape most potential predators.

RABBITS You'll probably see several species of rabbits while visiting Bryce Canyon and Zion National Parks. **Black-tailed jackrabbits,** easily recognized by their tall ears and black tails, are observed frequently along the cliffs at the rim of Bryce Canyon, and throughout Zion. Usually gaunt-looking, with mostly gray fur, they have large hind feet. The cute **desert cottontails** are also found at both parks, although mostly at Zion in grasslands below 5,000 feet of elevation. Desert cottontails are usually a brownish gray, with black-tipped ears and a trademark tail that looks just like a little white ball of cotton. Both species are favorite foods of the coyote.

RINGTAIL Also known as miner's cats or Ringtail cats, Ringtails are not cats at all, but relatives of the raccoon. They have foxlike faces, with big, round, dark eyes, but their most conspicuous feature is their long, bushy, black-and-white tail. The Ringtail

9

A NATURE GUIDE | The Fauna

Black-Tailed Jackrabbit

Desert Cottontail

is usually about 30 inches long, and often more than half of that length is tail. Although common in Zion and present, although not in abundance, at Bryce Canyon, Ringtails are seldom seen because they sleep all day in caves or other quiet places and emerge only after dark, when their super-sharp claws and catlike agility enable them to catch rodents, small mammals,

Ringtail

birds, and insects. They are also not above raiding campsites. Ringtails got the nickname "miner's cats" because, in the late 1800s and early 1900s, they were taken into mines, where they quickly eliminated the mouse and rat populations.

SQUIRRELS Practically every visitor to Zion and Bryce Canyon National Parks will see squirrels—at Zion, there's an abundance of **white-tailed antelope** and **rock squirrels,** while the most commonly seen species at Bryce Canyon is the **golden-mantled ground squirrel,** although there are plenty of rock and **red squirrels** as well. Often confused with chipmunks, which are generally the same size, shape, and coloring as squirrels, they are really quite easy to tell apart—chipmunks have stripes on the sides of their faces and squirrels do not. The golden-mantled ground squirrel, which seems to think it owns the Bryce Canyon campgrounds, is especially attractive, with a white stripe bordered by two black stripes along each side of its brownish-gray body, and reddish-brown or copper-colored head and shoulders.

Squirrel

Birds

AMERICAN DIPPER Also called water ouzels, these birds are seen year-round in the Narrows at Zion National Park, where they dive into the Virgin River in search of aquatic insects. Mostly slate-gray, with a stocky build, short tail, and wings, they run along the river bottom underwater, and in shallow areas appear to be water-skiing on the surface.

American Dipper

Mountain Chickadee

Bald Eagle

Golden Eagle

CHICKADEE Mountain chickadees are abundant year-round at Bryce Canyon, both below the rim and throughout the ponderosa pine forest, up to 8,500 feet of elevation. In Zion, you'll find them in the piñon-juniper forest, such as along Watchman Trail, as well as in the higher elevations. These small birds—only about 5 inches long—have pale, gray backs, jet-black caps and eye bands, and white cheeks, eyebrows, and chests.

EAGLES Both **golden** and **bald eagles** are seen fairly frequently at Bryce Canyon, especially near the cliffs along the rim. Both are occasionally seen at Zion, where golden eagles are sometimes spotted in the canyons and on the plateaus, while bald eagles are more commonly seen near water, including the Virgin River and its tributaries. Both species are large, with wingspans usually over 6 feet. The golden eagle is dark—brown and black—with light gold on the back of its neck. The bald eagle looks much like the golden eagle when young, but it develops a white head and tail and a more solidly black body as it matures. Bald eagles have yellow bills, which are larger than the

dark gray bills of golden eagles. While golden eagles eat rabbits and
large rodents, bald eagles generally prefer fish, which is why they
are usually seen near bodies of water. A few golden eagles are year-
round residents of both parks; fall through spring is the best time
to see bald eagles. (See also "Turkey Vulture," later in the chapter.)

HERON   Large birds with long legs and necks, **great blue herons** are ideally suited for wading in the reservoirs and rivers of Zion
National Park in search of a fish dinner.
They will also eat insects, smaller birds,
and rodents. They are sometimes seen as
they migrate through the area in spring or
fall. Great blue herons often stand over 4
feet tall, and have wingspans of almost 6
feet. In color, however, they are not really
blue but mostly gray, with some black and
white. They have a long, pointed yellow
bill. Occasionally they are also seen in or
near Bryce Canyon National Park.

Great Blue Heron

HUMMINGBIRDS   These colorful little birds are delightful to watch, as they
hover at flowers sipping nectar, perform
rambunctious aerial mating dances, or warn other hummingbirds
away with tail-fanning and other displays. (You might also notice
that hummingbirds can fly backward—they're the only birds
known to do this.) Among the species at Zion are the **black-
chinned, Costa's, broad-tailed,** and **rufous;** while at Bryce
Canyon, you will most likely see the black-chinned and broad-
tailed, although rufous are occasionally spotted. The most colorful
among these are the rufous: The males are a startling reddish-
brown with an iridescent red-orange throat, while females have
green backs with areas of reddish-brown on their tails and flanks.

9

A NATURE GUIDE | The Fauna

Black-Chinned Hummingbird   *Broad-Tailed Hummingbird*

JAYS   Among the noisiest and most raucous-sounding birds, jays are almost always heard before they are seen, although because of their size—sometimes a foot long—these year-round residents of both parks are easy to spot as well. **Scrub jays,** seen at numerous locations at both Zion and Bryce Canyon, often have a brilliant blue back, white or gray underneath, and a black mask. **Steller's Jays** are bright blue on their lower half and flat black above, with a prominent crest on the top of their heads. **Piñon jays** are deep blue, almost all over, with a bit of white on their throats and possibly other markings.

Steller's Jay

Scrub Jay

NUTHATCHES   Seen year-round throughout both Bryce Canyon and Zion, especially at higher elevations, Nuthatches are known for their ability to walk down tree trunks with their heads aimed straight down. The **white-breasted Nuthatch** is the species most commonly spotted at Zion, sometimes along the upper sections of the West Rim Trail or in the Kolob Canyon area; it's also seen in various locations throughout Bryce Canyon. A white-breasted Nuthatch is about 6 inches long, with a blue back; a white face, chest, and belly; and a black cap on its head. The **pygmy Nuthatch** is commonly seen in the ponderosa pine forests in Bryce and occasionally observed in Zion. This tiny bird, rarely more than 4½ inches from the tip of its beak to the tip of its tail,

Piñon Jay   *Pygmy Nuthatch*

is bluish-gray on its back and sides, white or light gray underneath, and has a dark cap on its head. Also frequently seen at Bryce Canyon—generally in the forests above 8,500 feet—but only occasionally at Zion, are **red-breasted Nuthatches,** which, not surprisingly, are recognized by their red or rust-colored chests. They have blue-gray backs and dark crowns, plus white eyebrows and a dark line behind each eye.

PEREGRINE FALCON Fairly common along the cliffs just below the rim at Bryce Canyon, and occasionally seen at Zion, peregrine falcons have wingspans that often exceed 3 feet, which helps make them one of the world's fastest birds, able to exceed 200 mph. They're known to breed at Zion and sometimes nest in the Weeping Rock area. Their back and wings are usually slate-gray or blue-gray, and this color projects vertically down their face in bands over their eyes. The rest of their face and neck is a light gray or white, and underneath, these falcons are usually a medium gray. During peregrine falcon nesting, which takes place from early spring to July, some areas at Zion National Park are off-limits to rock climbers. Pesticides drastically reduced the number of peregrine falcons in America in the 1950s and 1960s; and by 1970, there were only 39 breeding pairs known to exist in the continental United States. But after years on the endangered species list, they are on the increase again, thanks to a ban on many pesticides; in 1999, there were sufficient numbers of the birds that they were removed from the list. Interestingly, you'll also see peregrines in cities, where they nest on tall buildings or bridges and dine on pigeons.

Peregrine Falcon

Tip for Wildlife Watchers

Although it's generally true that you'll see most animals—especially mammals—early and late in the day, finding a quiet spot can be almost as important. For instance, you're likely to see **mule deer** in Watchman Campground, at Zion, in midday. When practically all the campers have left for the trails or scenic drives, the deer take advantage of the quiet to stop in for a drink in the river.

RED-TAILED HAWK   Year-round residents of both Bryce Canyon and Zion, red-tailed hawks are always on the lookout for small

Red-Tailed Hawk

rodents, the mainstay of their diet. They're often seen as they glide over open areas in search of prey— watch for them over the hoodoos in Bryce Canyon—or perch in a tree at the edge of a meadow, watching for any movement in the grass. Stocky, with wingspans of about 4 feet, red-tails are named for their rust-colored tails. Their chests and faces are usually white, and their upper parts are variable, from light to dark brown.

SWALLOWS   Known for their long, pointed wings and superb grace while flying, flocks of swallows are often seen in both parks during the summer, soaring over the meadows and plateaus, and along the cliffs at the rim of Bryce Canyon. The most commonly

Cliff Swallow

seen species are **violet-green swallows**—pretty little birds with striking, metallic-green backs, bright violet on their tails, and white faces and lower parts. Also watch for **cliff swallows** in both parks, not only near cliffs but also in the woods along the Virgin River at Zion. Cliff swallows have mostly blue-gray upper parts, with white below, but also often have dark auburn throats and foreheads.

SWIFTS   This speedy bird (hence the name) not only catches and consumes its dinner of insects while flying, but also never perches, clinging instead to trees trunks and other vertical surfaces.

Violet-Green Swallow   *White-Throated Swift*

White-throated swifts are found during the summer in the canyons and cliffs at both Zion and Bryce Canyon, often in the same areas as violet-green swallows (see above). White-throated swifts are basically black and white—the wings, tail, and top of the head are black; the lower face, throat, and most of the chest are white.

TURKEY VULTURE   Birders in both Zion and Bryce Canyon have reported sightings of turkey vultures, also called buzzards, which are about the same size as eagles and, when flying, are sometimes mistaken for golden eagles. The main visual difference is that the turkey vulture has a red head, and, unlike the golden eagle, it can glide seemingly forever without flapping its wings, riding on columns of warm air known as thermals.

Reptiles & Amphibians

CANYON TREE FROG   Often camouflaged among rocks near pools and streams in Zion National Park's side canyons, the canyon tree frog is generally olive, gray, or brown, with indistinct dark patches on its back. From 1¼ to 2¼ inches long, it often has a light spot below its eye. During the spring mating season, you can often hear a lively chorus of tree frogs.

Turkey Vulture

Canyon Tree Frog

GREAT BASIN RATTLESNAKE   A subspecies of the Western Rattlesnake, the Great Basin Rattlesnake is found both above and below the rim at Bryce Canyon, and in most areas of Zion. Generally they hibernate in winter, so you will most likely encounter

Rattlesnake

them only April through October. Sometimes growing to more than 5 feet long, they are usually gray or light brown with dark patches on their backs. They have wide, triangular-shaped flat heads, and bony, interlocking segments on their tails, which produce a buzzing or hissing noise when shaken—this usually happens when the snake is agitated. Each time the snake sheds its skin, which can occur up to five times a year, the rattle gets a new segment. These snakes are highly poisonous, but usually only attack humans when they feel threatened. Because they are mainly nocturnal, those walking in isolated areas at night should use flashlights to avoid stepping on them.

Short-Horned Lizard

MOUNTAIN SHORT-HORNED LIZARD These little lizards—usually between 2 and 4 inches long—are found in abundance in a variety of habitats in Bryce Canyon National Park and at higher elevations at Zion. They are active mostly during the day, and their diet consists mainly of ants, but they will also eat other insects and even small snakes. Mountain short-horned lizards have a broad, flat body, short tail, and short horns on the back of their heads. They are usually reddish brown, with darker spots on their backs.

NORTHERN SAGEBRUSH LIZARD Commonly seen on trails below the rim at Bryce Canyon National Park and in the dry, open areas of rocks and sagebrush at Zion, the northern sagebrush lizard is slim, at least compared to the mountain short-horned lizard discussed above, and brown to grayish-green in color; the males have blue markings on their bellies. This lizard may also have stripes of various shades of brown or light tan running the length of its body.

Invertebrates

ZION SNAIL One creature unique to Zion National Park is the Zion snail, which you'll only find clinging to wet canyon walls in a 4-mile section of the Narrows along the Virgin River—the Riverside Walk as it enters the Narrows is a good place to see them. The walls are kept moist by seeps and springs, which also nurture hanging gardens. This tiny snail, complete with shell, is a mere eighth of an inch or less across, and to the naked eye appears to be just a dark brown or black speck on a shiny, wet wall. They hold onto the slick walls with a suction-cup foot, which in proportion to the creature's size is the biggest foot of any snail, a phenomenon that has caused some park rangers to refer to the Zion snail as "our little bigfoot." Please do not attempt to touch these fragile creatures.

THE ECOSYSTEM

So far, Zion and Bryce Canyon National Parks have managed to escape most of the serious ecological problems that plague some of America's other national parks, such as air and water pollution from nearby cities, adjacent mining, and extreme overcrowding (with its resultant air and noise pollution from automobiles). Still, there is the threat of air pollution from power plants across the Colorado Plateau, and the park service has concerns over how Bryce Canyon and Zion national parks can be best managed to both preserve their delicate ecosystems and produce a rewarding experience for park visitors.

Presently, visitors to both Zion and Bryce Canyon can still get away from humanity fairly easily by heading out onto park trails or into the backcountry, and they can still find relatively unspoiled areas there. To preserve these unspoiled areas and their ecosystems, increasing efforts are being made in both parks to make visitors understand the need for zero-impact visitation, or as close as people can get to zero-impact short of staying home. In most cases, people are getting the message and are doing their best to stay on trails, not pollute water or drop trash, and certainly not to disturb the parks' plants and animals. In addition, shuttle bus systems have been implemented at both parks to help relieve traffic congestion and parking problems.

One issue that is expected to take on more importance in the years to come—and over which the National Park Service has little control—is increasing development in nearby communities. Major hotels have been built just outside Zion; and some degradation to Bryce Canyon's delightful night sky is feared from continuing development just outside that park's entrance.

Meanwhile, within park boundaries the main issue—both now and for the future—is overcrowding, and how it affects the variety of habitats that support a vast array of plant and animal life. Officials of the National Park Service have taken the position that they do not want to limit the number of people who visit the parks, and have concluded that the problem isn't too many people, it's too many cars. So now we're seeing limitations and even outright bans on private motor vehicles in the parks, especially during their busiest seasons.

Visitation at many national parks, including Bryce Canyon, has seen ups and downs over the past 10 to 12 years. (An exception is

Zion, which has generally seen annual increases.) However, the long-term trend is expected to be increasing visitation and park managers are rightly concerned about the future.

The issue of how the parks can handle an increasing number of visitors brings to mind the question of the entire philosophy of the National Park Service, which essentially is to accomplish two goals simultaneously—preserve resources and promote visitor enjoyment. But which is more important: protecting the plants, animals, and geologic formations that make these parks the special places they are, or helping people enjoy these very same plants, animals, and geologic formations?

Essentially, the question is how far should parks go to accommodate their visitors—the people who pay the entrance and user fees and in most cases the tax dollars that fund the parks—and at what point does visitor impact become unacceptable? It's a tightrope for park managers and a debate both within and outside the park service that will not be settled soon, if ever.

PLANNING YOUR TRIP TO ZION & BRYCE CANYON NATIONAL PARKS

There once was a time when planning a visit to a national park involved little more than choosing the dates and packing the car. Yet as more people discover the parks, it becomes harder to secure campsites, lodging, and even parking. To combat this, it's best to decide what you want to do at the park and then try to schedule your visit for the least-crowded time that is best for those activities. So, if horseback riding is something you want to do, schedule your trip for spring or fall, when the stables are open but the crowds are few.

Luckily, there are more lodging and dining choices in and near the national parks than there were 20 or 25 years ago. At that time, we were happy if we found a restaurant that was clean and served basic American food.

GETTING THERE

Zion and Bryce Canyon national parks, located in rural southern Utah, are not close to any major cities or transportation hubs, and the vast majority of visitors will arrive by car, either their own or a rental. Those not driving their own vehicles will likely fly to one of several cities or towns and rent a car for the remainder of their trip. The parks are 83 miles apart by road.

Attention visitors to the U.S. from abroad: Some major airlines offer transatlantic or transpacific passengers special discount tickets under the name **Visit USA,** which allows mostly one-way travel from one U.S. destination to another at very low prices. Unavailable in the U.S., these discount tickets must be purchased abroad in conjunction with your international fare. This system is the easiest, fastest, cheapest way to see the country. Inquire with your air carrier.

If you plan to rent a car in the United States, keep in mind that foreign driver's licenses are usually recognized in the U.S., but you may want to consider obtaining an international driver's license. International visitors should also note that insurance and taxes are almost never included in quoted rental car rates in the U.S. And, when putting fuel in your vehicle, be aware that taxes are already included in the printed price. One U.S. gallon equals 3.8 liters or .85 imperial gallons.

Getting to Zion National Park

Zion National Park is located 46 miles northeast of St. George, 60 miles south of Cedar City, 83 miles southwest of Bryce Canyon National Park, and 120 miles northwest of the north rim of Grand Canyon National Park, in northern Arizona. It's 309 miles south of Salt Lake City and 158 miles northeast of Las Vegas, Nevada.

By Plane

There are small airports at St. George (Airport Code SGU; ☎ 435/627-4080; www.flysgu.com) and Cedar City (Airport Code CDC; ☎ 435/867-9408; www.cedarcity.org), both located along I-15. At this time the St. George airport offers service on **Delta** (☎ 800/221-1212; www.delta.com), with flights to and from Salt Lake City, and **United** (☎ 800/864-8331; www.united.com), with flights to and from Los Angeles. The Cedar City airport is also served by **Delta,** with flights to and from Salt Lake City (See contact information above.) From either airport, it's easy to rent a car and drive to Zion. Several major car-rental agencies serve each airport.

The closest major airport to Zion is McCarran International Airport in Las Vegas, Nevada (Airport Code LAS; ☎ 702/261-5211; www.mccarran.com), which is about 120 miles southwest of St. George via I-15. Most major airlines fly into McCarran, and most major car-rental agencies have outlets at the airport.

The **St. George Shuttle** (☎ 800/933-8320 or 435/628-8320; www.stgshuttle.com) provides daily service between St. George and the Las Vegas airport for $30 per person one-way or $50 round trip (2 hr. 10 min. each way).

By Bus

Greyhound (© **800/231-2222** in the U.S.; © **001/214/849-8100** outside the U.S. with toll-free access; www.greyhound.com) is the sole nationwide bus line. It provides service to St. George and Cedar City, Utah, and Las Vegas, Nevada. See "By Plane," above for transportation from those cities to Zion National Park.

International visitors can obtain the **Greyhound North American Discovery Pass.** It offers unlimited travel and stopovers in the U.S. and Canada, and can be obtained outside the United States from travel agents or through www.discoverypass.com.

By Car

From St. George, travel north on I-15 10 miles to exit 16, then east on Utah 9 for 30 miles to the Zion Canyon section of the park. From Salt Lake City take I-15 south to exit 27, then Utah 17 south about 10 miles, and Utah 9 east about 20 miles. Though less scenic than the eastern approach to the park, this is the easiest route; it's more direct, avoids possible delays at the Zion–Mt. Carmel Tunnel, and delivers you to Springdale, just outside the park's southern entrance, where most of the area's lodging and restaurants are located. (See chapter 4, "Where to Stay, Camp & Eat in Zion.")

The Kolob Canyons section, in the park's northwest corner, is reached via the short Kolob Canyons Road, off I-15, exit 40.

From the east, it's a spectacularly scenic 24-mile drive from Mt. Carmel Junction, on Utah 9 (the Zion–Mt. Carmel Hwy.), reached from either north or south via U.S. 89. However, be aware that this route into the park drops over 2,500 feet in elevation, passes through the mile-long Zion–Mt. Carmel Tunnel, and winds down six steep switchbacks. Oversize vehicles are charged $15 for use of the tunnel. (See "Regulations" in chapter 2, "Exploring Zion National Park.") From this approach, you'll end up on the Zion Canyon Scenic Drive and then at the visitor center.

Bryce Canyon National Park is north and east of Mt. Carmel Junction via U.S. 89 north (44 miles) and Utah 12 east (13 miles). Kanab is 17 miles southeast of Mt. Carmel Junction along U.S. 89.

Getting to Bryce Canyon National Park

Bryce Canyon National Park is 50 miles west of Escalante, 80 miles east of Cedar City, 83 miles northeast of Zion National Park, 120 miles southwest of Capitol Reef National Park, 135 miles northeast of St. George, and 160 miles north of the north rim of Grand Canyon National Park in northern Arizona. It's about 250 miles south of Salt Lake City.

By Plane

The closest airport with regularly scheduled service is at Cedar City, and also fairly close is the airport at St. George. In addition, you can fly to Las Vegas, Nevada, and rent a car; or take a shuttle from there to St. George, where you can also rent a car. These options are discussed above, in "Getting to Zion National Park."

Bryce Canyon Airport (Airport Code BCE; ☎ **435/834-5239;** www.brycecanyonairport.com), at 7,586 feet of elevation, is several miles from the park entrance on Utah 12, and has a 7,400-foot lighted runway. There is no regularly scheduled airline service, but charter service is available from **Bryce Canyon Airlines** (☎ **435/834-8060;** www.rubysinn.com/bryce-canyon-airlines.html). A free shuttle services local motels, and car rentals are available from **Hertz** (☎ **800/654-3131;** www.hertz.com), at the Chevron at Ruby's Inn.

By Bus

See "Getting to Zion National Park," above.

By Car

From Zion National Park, head east on Utah 9 about 18 miles to U.S. 89, north 44 miles to Utah 12, and east 17 miles to the park entrance road (Utah 63). Then go 3 miles south on Utah 63 to reach the park entrance.

From St. George, travel north on I-15 10 miles to exit 16, east on Utah 9 for 63 miles to U.S. 89, north 44 miles to Utah 12, and then east 17 miles on Utah 12 to the park entrance road.

From Capitol Reef National Park, take Utah 24 west 10 miles to Torrey, turn southwest onto Scenic Highway Utah 12, and drive for about 110 miles, passing through the towns of Boulder and Escalante, to the park entrance road.

From Salt Lake City, take I-15 south about 200 miles to exit 95, east 13 miles on Utah 20, south on U.S. 89 for 17 miles to Utah 12, and east 17 miles on Utah 12 to the park entrance road.

GETTING AROUND

At either Zion or Bryce Canyon national parks there are two main ways to get around—private vehicle and/or shuttle bus. Due to road congestion within the parks, both have instituted shuttle buses from late spring through early fall in the most popular areas of the parks. At Zion, it's mandatory—private vehicles are

Getting Around

PLANNING YOUR TRIP

Southern Utah Driving Times & Distances

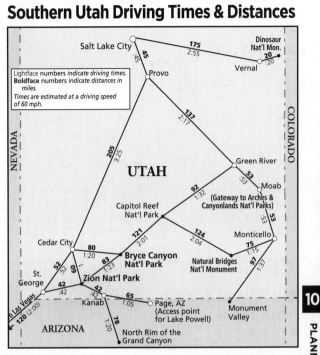

Lightface numbers *indicate driving times.*
Boldface numbers *indicate distances in miles.*
Times are estimated at a driving speed of 60 mph.

Salt Lake City

175 2:55 Dinosaur Nat'l Mon.

20 .20 Vernal

45 .45 Provo

COLORADO

137 2:17

205 3:25

UTAH

Green River

53 .53 Moab
(Gateway to Arches & Canyonlands Nat'l Parks)

92 1:32

Capitol Reef Nat'l Park

121 2:01

124 2:04

53 .53

Monticello

NEVADA

Cedar City

80 1:20

Bryce Canyon Nat'l Park

Natural Bridges Nat'l Monument

75 1:15

97 1:37

52 .52

83 1:23

60 .60

Zion Nat'l Park

St. George

42 .42

42 .42

Kanab

65 1:05

Page, AZ
(Access point for Lake Powell)

Monument Valley

To Las Vegas

120 (2:00)

ARIZONA

78 1:20

North Rim of the Grand Canyon

prohibited on the park road when the shuttle is running; at Bryce Canyon, use of the shuttle bus is optional. Unlimited use of the shuttle buses in both parks is included in the entrance fee.

Getting Around Zion National Park
BY CAR

Most visitors to Zion will be arriving at the South Entrance, at the town of Springdale. From April through October private vehicle use in this area is limited and visitors must use the shuttle on the Zion Canyon Scenic Drive. The rest of the year you are free to drive yourself on the scenic drive. However, there is no shuttle and you are free to drive yourself year-round along the Zion-Mount Carmel Highway (from the park's East Entrance) and in the Kolob Canyons and Terrace sections of the park. See "Essentials," p. 17, and "Seeing the Park by Car & Shuttle," p. 27.

Year-round fuel stations include **Springdale Chevron,** on the south side of town, at 1593 Zion Park Blvd. (© **435/772-3677**). Outside the park's east entrance, there is a gas station at 4490 S.

State St., Mt. Carmel (☎ **435/648-2326**). Emergency 24-hour service is available from **W. J. Bassett Repair** (☎ **435/772-3328**), in Springdale.

BY SHUTTLE

The park's shuttle bus system runs from April through October, and during that time access to Zion Canyon Scenic Drive (above Utah 9) is limited to shuttle buses, hikers, and bikers. The only exceptions are overnight Zion Lodge guests and tour buses connected with the lodge, which have access to the road as far as the lodge. The shuttle system consists of two loops: one in the town of Springdale and the other along Zion Canyon Scenic Drive, with the loops connecting at the transit/visitor center just inside the south park entrance. Shuttle stops are located at all the major-use areas in the park, and shuttles run frequently (about every 6 min. at peak times). The buses are handicap accessible. From November through March, when park visitation is lowest, visitors are permitted to drive the full length of Zion Canyon Scenic Drive in their own vehicles. Complete information about the shuttle and all stops is available at the visitor center. Also see "Seeing the Park by Car & Shuttle," p. 27.

Getting Around Bryce Canyon National Park

BY CAR

Getting around Bryce Canyon National Park is simple: there's one road, and it's a dead-end. Although the park is crossed east-west along its north edge by Utah 12, most of the park—including the visitor center and most of the things you want to see—are accessed by Utah 63, which turns south off Utah 12 and becomes the park's 18-mile (one-way) scenic drive. You can take your own vehicle on the scenic drive at any time, although use of the shuttle is recommended. See "Seeing the Park by Car," p. 76.

Just outside the entrance to the park, **American Car Care Center & Bryce Canyon Towing** (☎ **435/835-5232**) is a full-service station, with gasoline and diesel fuel. It has facilities to work on large vehicles and motor homes and provides AAA towing services. There are also gas stations along Utah 12 in the communities of Bryce (where Utah 63 turns south off Utah 12) and Tropic (along Utah 12, about 8 miles east of Bryce).

BY SHUTTLE

To alleviate traffic congestion during the busy summer season, a voluntary shuttle service runs daily from early May through early October. Visitors can park their cars at the parking and boarding area at the intersection of the entrance road and Utah 12, 3 miles from the park boundary, and ride the shuttle into the park. The shuttle has stops at various viewpoints, as well as at Ruby's Inn, Ruby's Campground, the visitor center, Sunset Campground, and the Lodge at Bryce Canyon. The shuttle runs every 12 to 15 minutes and is handicap accessible. See "Seeing the Park by Shuttle," p. 77.

EXPLORING THE PARKS BY RV OR "CAR-CAMPING"

One of the best ways to explore Zion and Bryce parks is in an RV, or in a car or truck while spending your nights in a tent.

There are a few things that RVers might want to know. Entering Zion from the east in an RV involves an extra fee and maybe a short wait to get through the Zion–Mt. Carmel Tunnel, and there may be parking restrictions along the Zion Canyon Scenic Drive. However, entering the park from this direction is worth it, and taking your RV into these parks isn't much of a hassle, especially if you plan ahead.

Parking is limited, especially for motor homes and other large vehicles, so park your RV where you'll be camping, and take shuttle buses as much as possible. Drive either early or late in the day, when there's less traffic—the best times to explore the parks anyway.

If you'll be traveling in the parks in your RV and want to make it obvious that your campsite is occupied, carry something to leave in it, such as a cardboard box with "Site Taken" clearly written on it.

Because many of the national park campsites are not level, carry four or five short boards, or leveling blocks, to place under the RV's wheels. You can buy inexpensive levels at RV and hardware stores.

Elsewhere in this book you'll find information on camping in Zion and Bryce Canyon national parks, on nearby federal and state lands, and in the parks' gateway towns. Those planning to camp elsewhere in the state can get information on Utah's national forests from the **U.S. Forest Service Intermountain Region Office,** 324 25th St., Ogden, UT 84401 (📞 **801/625-5306;** www.fs.fed. us/r4). The Utah State Office of the **U.S. Bureau of Land Management** is at 440 W. 200 South, Ste. 500, Salt Lake City, UT 84145-0155 (📞 **801/539-4001;** www.blm.gov/ut). For information on Utah's state parks, contact **Utah State Parks,** 1594 W.

10

PLANNING YOUR TRIP

Exploring the Parks

RENTING AN rv FOR YOUR NATIONAL PARK TREK

If you own an RV, you're all set for a trip to Zion and Bryce Canyon National Parks; but if you don't, you might want to consider renting one.

But first, let's get one thing straight: You probably won't save a lot of money. It is possible to travel fairly cheaply if you limit your equipment to a tent, a pop-up tent trailer, or a small pickup truck camper, but renting a motor home will probably end up costing almost as much as driving a compact car, staying in moderately priced motels, and eating in family-style restaurants and cafes. That's because the motor home will go only one-third as far on a gallon of gas or diesel as your car, and they're expensive to rent (generally $1,000–$1,500 per week in midsummer).

But carrying your house with you let's you stay in relative comfort in the national park campgrounds, which many park visitors feel is one of the highlights of their trip. It also lets you stop for meals anytime and anywhere you choose, and you won't spend time searching for a restroom.

If you plan to fly into the area and rent an RV when you arrive, choose your starting point carefully. Rental rates are usually less in Las Vegas, Nevada, than in Salt Lake City, and most of Utah's national parks are closer to Vegas than to SLC anyway.

The country's largest RV rental company, with outlets in Las Vegas and Salt Lake City, is **Cruise America** (© **800/671-8042;** www.cruiseamerica.com). RV rentals are also available from **El Monte RV** (© **888/337-2214;** www.elmonterv.com) and **Camping World** (© **877/297-3687;** www.rvrental.com). Information on rental agencies, as well as tips on renting, can be obtained from the **Recreation Vehicle Rental Association** (www.rvra.org).

North Temple, Ste. 116, Salt Lake City, UT 84116 (© **877/887-2757** or 801/538-7220; www.stateparks.utah.gov).

Members of the **American Automobile Association (AAA)** can request the club's free *Southwestern CampBook,* which includes campgrounds and RV parks in Utah, Arizona, Colorado, and New Mexico; and several good national and regional campground guides are also available.

TIPS ON ACCOMMODATIONS

The small towns that serve as gateways to Zion and Bryce Canyon national parks, as well as the parks themselves, offer a varied but

PASSES OFFER free admission ON MOST FEDERAL LANDS

Those who enjoy vacationing at national parks, national forests, and other federal lands have opportunities to save quite a bit of money by using the federal government's annual passes. The ***America the Beautiful—National Parks and Federal Recreational Lands Pass*** costs $80 for 1 year, from the date of purchase, for the general public. It provides free admission for the pass holder, and those in his or her vehicle, to recreation sites that charge vehicle entrance fees on lands administered by the National Park Service, U.S. Forest Service, U.S. Fish and Wildlife Service, Bureau of Land Management, and Bureau of Reclamation. At areas that charge per-person fees, the passes are good for the pass holder, plus three additional adults. Children 15 and under are admitted free.

The passes are also available for U.S. citizens and permanent residents ages 62 and older for a lifetime fee of $10 (Senior Pass), and are free for U.S. residents and permanent residents with disabilities (Access Pass). The Senior and Access passes also provide 50% discounts on some fees, such as those for camping. The Senior and Access passes can be obtained by mail with an application form available online (see below) with a $10 processing fee, or without the processing fee in person at national parks, U.S. Forest Service offices, and other federal recreation sites. The general public version (the $80 one) can be purchased in person, by phone (© **888/275-8747**, ext. 1), or online at http://store.usgs.gov/pass.

somewhat limited selection of lodging possibilities. Both parks have handsome lodges and cabins, owned by the National Park Service and managed by concessionaires. Rates for the park lodges are controlled by the park service and are not outrageous.

Outside the parks you'll find chain motels, independent mom-and-pop motels, and a few small bed and breakfasts, often in historic homes. Rates vary, but these towns are tourist traps, and you are unlikely to find bargains, especially during the busy summer season. Resist the temptation and stay in or as close to the parks as you can afford.

The best—and perhaps only—way to really save money on lodging is to go in the off season, preferably just before or just after the high season. We recently spent a week at Zion National Park in late March. The cool, spring weather was perfect for hiking and lodging cost close to half of June or July rates.

PACKAGE & ADVENTURE TOURS

A number of nationally recognized companies offer tours that include Zion and Bryce and surrounding areas. In most cases, all you do is pay, and then the outfitters arrange everything, including lodging, meals, and transportation. Offerings range from fairly standard bus tours to luxury adventure vacations. You'll want to contact tour operators as far in advance as possible, as reservations are required and group sizes are limited. The adventure tour operators generally specialize in small groups and have trips for various levels of ability and physical fitness. Trips are offered in a range of price categories, from basic to luxurious, and are of varying lengths.

For a list of outfitters in Utah, as well as a lot of other useful information and Web links, contact the **Utah Office of Tourism,** Council Hall, 300 N. State St., Salt Lake City, UT 84114 (© **800/ 200-1160;** www.utah.com), or check out the website of **Utah Guides & Outfitters,** www.utah-adventures.com.

In addition to the companies listed below, one well-respected national company that offers tours to southern Utah's national parks is **Tauck Tours** (© **800/788-7885;** www.tauck.com). A good online source for a variety of outdoor adventure trips offered by various outfitters is **www.adventurefinder.com**.

- **Austin-Lehman Adventures,** P.O. Box 81025, Billings, MT 59108-1025 (© **800/575-1540** or 406/655-4591; www.austin lehman.com), offers guided multiday hiking tours in Zion and Bryce Canyon national parks and surrounding areas.
- **Backroads,** 801 Cedar St., Berkeley, CA 94710-1800 (© **800/ 462-2848** or 510/527-1555; www.backroads.com), offers a variety of guided multiday road biking, mountain biking, and hiking tours in Zion and Bryce Canyon.
- **Bicycle Adventures,** 29700 SE High Point Way, Issaquah, WA 98027 (© **800/443-6060** or 425/250-5540; www.bicycle adventures.com), offers guided multiday hiking and biking excursions in Zion and Bryce Canyon national parks.
- **REI Adventures,** P.O. Box 1938, Sumner, WA 98390 (© **800/622-2236** or 253/437-1100; www.rei.com/adventures), offers guided multiday hiking and biking treks into Zion and Bryce Canyon national parks, plus a unique trip on New Year's Day that includes a bit of snowshoeing with your hike.
- **The World Outdoors,** 2840 Wilderness Place, Ste. D, Boulder, CO 80301 (© **800/488-8483** or 303/413-0946; www.theworld outdoors.com), offers a variety of trips, including hiking and multisport adventures to Zion and Bryce Canyon national parks.

PLANNING YOUR TRIP | Package & Adventure Tours

TIPS FOR TRAVELERS WITH PETS

Although national surveys show that about two-thirds of pet owners take their pets along on their travels, practically all national parks, including Zion and Bryce Canyon, are not pet-friendly; therefore, those planning to visit the parks should consider leaving their pets at home. Pets are prohibited on hiking trails, in the backcountry, and in all buildings, and must always be on a leash no more than 6 feet long. One happy exception is at Zion, where leashed pets are permitted on the Pa'rus Trail. Pets should not be left unattended in campgrounds at either park. Essentially, this means that if you take your pet into the parks they can be with you in the campgrounds and inside your vehicle, and you can walk them in parking areas, but that's about it.

Pets should **never** be left in closed vehicles, where temperatures can soar to over 120°F (49°C) in minutes, resulting in brain damage or death. Outside Bryce Canyon National Park, in Tropic, **Canyon Park Animal Retreat** (© **435/679-8548**) offers day boarding; and in Panguitch, about 30 miles west, day and overnight boarding are available at **Pawzdogz** (© **436/691-3696;** www.pawzdogz.com). Visitors to Zion National Park will find day and overnight pet boarding in the community of Rockville, just a few miles from the park, at **Doggy Dude Ranch** (© **435/772-3105;** www.doggyduderanch.com).

Those who do decide to take pets with them into these parks, despite the fact that they are not permitted in most places, should take their pets' leashes (of course); carry plenty of water (pet shops and outdoor equipment suppliers sell clever little travel water bowls); and bring proof that their dogs or cats have been vaccinated against rabies. Flea and tick spray or powder is also important, especially if you will be taking your pet to Bryce Canyon, where bubonic plague is transmitted by the fleas that prey on

10

Special Tip for Pet Owners

Although pets are not permitted on practically any of the trails or in the backcountry in Bryce Canyon and Zion national parks, those traveling with their dogs can hike with them over miles of trails administered by the U.S. Forest Service and Bureau of Land Management, adjacent to both national parks. Pets are also welcome, even on trails, in Grand Staircase–Escalante National Monument (run by the BLM) and in Utah's state parks. (See chapter 8, "Nearby Things to See & Do.")

prairie dogs and other rodents. (See chapter 5, "Exploring Bryce Canyon National Park.") A good online source of information for pet owners is **www.petswelcome.com**.

HEALTH & SAFETY

The rugged landscapes that make Zion and Bryce Canyon such beautiful destinations can also be hazardous. Because many areas in the parks are isolated, there may be no one there to help in an emergency; and because the parks have spotty cell phone service—nonexistent in more remote areas—you should not count on being able to call for help. Always check with park offices and park rangers about current conditions before heading out.

Southern Utah's extremes of **climate**—from burning desert to snow-covered mountains—can produce health problems, if you're not prepared. If you haven't been to the desert before, it can be difficult to comprehend the heat, dryness, and intensity of the sun. If you're prone to dry skin, moisturizing lotion is a must; even if you're not, you will probably end up using it. Everyone needs to use a good quality sun block, wear a hat, and wear sunglasses with full ultraviolet protection. Hikers and others planning to be outside will also need to carry water—at least a gallon per person per day.

The other potential problem is **elevation.** Bryce Canyon National Park rises to over 9,000 feet, and a side trip to Cedar Breaks National Monument will take you to over 10,000 feet. (See chapter 8, "Nearby Things to See & Do.") These elevations are high enough to produce health problems for those not accustomed to them—there's less oxygen and lower humidity up there than many visitors are used to. In fact, the most common complaint at the first-aid station at the Lodge at Bryce Canyon is shortness of breath. Those with heart or respiratory problems should consult their doctors before planning a trip to these parks, Bryce Canyon in particular. If you're in generally good health, you don't need to take any special precautions, but it's advisable to ease into high elevations by changing altitude gradually. Also, get plenty of rest, avoid large meals, and drink plenty of nonalcoholic fluids, especially water.

State health officials also warn outdoor enthusiasts to take precautions against **hantavirus,** a rare but often fatal respiratory disease, first recognized in 1993. About half of the country's confirmed cases have been reported in the Four Corners states of Colorado, New Mexico, Arizona, and Utah. The droppings and urine of rodents usually spread the disease, and health officials recommend that campers and hikers avoid areas with signs of rodent occupation. Symptoms of hantavirus are similar to flu, and lead to breathing difficulties and shock.

A british **INVASION**

Only 60 miles north Cedar City is Utah's premier theater event—the highly acclaimed **Utah Shakespearean Festival** ★★★. The season, which runs from late June through late October, includes eight plays—usually three by Shakespeare and five others—in which top actors perform in true Elizabethan style in an open-air replica of the original Globe Theatre and in a modern enclosed theater. Recently scheduled productions include Shakespeare's *The Merry Wives of Windsor, Titus Andronicus,* and *Hamlet;* plus *Stones in His Pockets* by Marie Jones and *Death of a Mockingbird* by Christopher Sergel, based on the novel by Harper Lee.

You can also take a backstage tour for $8 per person, and a variety of other programs and special events are scheduled.

The festival is held on the Southern Utah University campus, 351 W. Center St., Cedar City, UT 84720. For tickets (which range from $22 to $71) and information, call ✆ **800/752-9849** or 435/586-7878; or visit www.bard.org.

Other park-specific problems are bubonic plague, which is discussed on p. 69, and flash flooding, which is discussed on p. 50.

PROTECTING THE ENVIRONMENT

Many of the wonderful outdoor areas that you'll be exploring in Zion and Bryce Canyon national parks are quite isolated, especially in the backcountry at Zion. Not long ago, the rule was to "leave only footprints"; these days, we're trying to do better and not leave even those. It's relatively easy to be a good outdoor citizen—pack out all trash, stay on established trails, be especially careful not to pollute water, and, in general, do your best to have as little impact on the environment as possible. Some hikers carry a small trash bag to pick up what others may have left. As the park service likes to remind us, protecting our national parks is everyone's responsibility.

[FastFACTS] ZION NATIONAL PARK

Area Codes   The area code is 435.

ATMs   An automated teller machine (ATM) is available in the park at Zion Lodge. There are also ATMs in Springdale, at **Sol Foods**

Supermarket & Deli, 95 Zion Park Blvd. (📞 **435/772-0277;** www.
solfoods.com), and there is also an ATM, as well as other banking
services, at **Zions Bank,** 921 Zion Park Blvd. (📞 **435/772-3274;**
www.zionsbank.com).

Car Rental See "Getting There by Car," earlier in this chapter.

Cellphones See "Mobile Phones," later in this section.

Disabled Travelers The National Park Service has made great
strides in recent years in making their facilities more accessible to
those with disabilities. Visitor centers at Zion are wheelchair accessible, including the restrooms. Accessible campsites are available in
South and Watchman campgrounds; Riverside Walk, at the end of
Zion Canyon Scenic Drive, is paved and accessible with assistance;
and Pa'rus Trail is a 2-mile paved and accessible trail, open also to
bicyclists. Zion's shuttle system is completely accessible. In addition,
park rangers are extremely receptive to helping visitors with disabilities. Disabled travelers can obtain free admission and discounts on
many park facilities, such as campgrounds. See "Passes Offer Free
Admission on Most Federal Lands," earlier in this chapter.

   The Utah information and referral line for people with disabilities is
📞 **800/333-8824,** or go online to www.accessut.org.

Doctors See "Medical Services," later in this section.

Drinking Laws The legal age for purchase and consumption of
alcoholic beverages is 21; proof of age is required and often
requested at bars, nightclubs, and restaurants, so it's always a good
idea to bring ID when you go out. Do not carry open containers of
alcohol in your car or any public area that isn't zoned for alcohol
consumption. Don't even think about driving while intoxicated.

Driving Rules See "Getting Around," earlier in this chapter.

Electricity Like Canada, the United States uses 110 to 120 volts
AC (60 cycles), compared to 220 to 240 volts AC (50 cycles) in
most of Europe, Australia, and New Zealand. Downward converters
that change 220–240 volts to 110–120 volts are difficult to find in
the United States, so bring one with you.

Embassies & Consulates All embassies are in the nation's capi-
tal, Washington, D.C. Some consulates are in major U.S. cities, and most
nations have a mission to the United Nations in New York City. If your
country isn't listed below, call for directory information in Washington,
D.C. (📞 **202/555-1212**) or check **www.embassy.org/embassies**.

   The embassy of **Australia** is at 1601 Massachusetts Ave. NW, Wash-
ington, DC 20036 (📞 **202/797-3000;** www.usa.embassy.gov.au).
Consulates are in New York, Honolulu, Houston, Los Angeles, and San
Francisco.

   The embassy of **Canada** is at 501 Pennsylvania Ave. NW, Washington, DC 20001 (📞 **202/682-1740;** www.canadainternational.gc.ca/

washington). Other Canadian consulates are in Buffalo (New York), Detroit, Los Angeles, New York, and Seattle.

The embassy of **Ireland** is at 2234 Massachusetts Ave. NW, Washington, DC 20008 (📞 **202/462-3939;** www.embassyofireland.org). Irish consulates are in Boston, Chicago, New York, San Francisco, and other cities. See website for complete listing.

The embassy of **New Zealand** is at 37 Observatory Circle NW, Washington, DC 20008 (📞 **202/328-4800;** www.nzembassy.com). New Zealand consulates are in Los Angeles, Salt Lake City, San Francisco, and Seattle.

The embassy of the **United Kingdom** is at 3100 Massachusetts Ave. NW, Washington, DC 20008 (📞 **202/588-6500;** http://ukinusa.fco.gov.uk). Other British consulates are in Atlanta, Boston, Chicago, Cleveland, Houston, Los Angeles, New York, San Francisco, and Seattle.

Emergencies   Dial 📞 **911** or 435/772-3322, 24 hours a day, or locate the nearest park ranger.

Family Travel   Visiting Zion National Park with your children can be an especially rewarding experience, and is an excellent way for everyone to learn about the park's geology, plants, and animals, as well as to appreciate the unequaled beauty of nature. In addition, Zion National Park has some of the best children's programs we've seen in any national parks.

However, the park is in a rural area, and the gateway towns offer the basics but little more. There are no major chain grocers or discount stores, and although you will be able to buy items such as baby food and disposable diapers, you may not find the variety that you're used to. Parents should stock up before they leave larger communities such as Las Vegas, Salt Lake City, or St. George. It's also a good idea to carry any prescription drugs you might need, and to have the phone numbers of your doctor and pharmacist.

To locate hotels, restaurants, and attractions that are particularly kid-friendly, look for the "Kids" icon throughout this guide.

Gasoline   See "Getting Around by Car," earlier in this chapter.

Health   See "Protecting Your Health & Safety," earlier in this chapter.

Hospitals   See "Medical Services," later in this section.

Insurance   For information on traveler's insurance, trip cancellation insurance, and medical insurance while traveling, please visit www.frommers.com/planning.

Internet & Wi-Fi   Free Wi-Fi access is available year-round in the lobby at Zion Lodge, and most lodging facilities discussed in chapter 4 also offer free Wi-Fi.

Laundry   There are no laundry facilities in Zion National Park, but coin-operated laundry machines and dryers are located at **Zion**

Canyon Campground (📞 **435/772-3237;** www.zioncamp.com), just outside the park's south entrance, and in downtown Springdale, in the **Zion Park Motel** complex, 865 Zion Park Blvd. (📞 **435/772-3251;** www.zionparkmotel.com).

Legal Aid   While driving, if you are pulled over for a minor infraction (such as speeding), never attempt to pay the fine directly to a police officer; this could be construed as attempted bribery, a much more serious crime. Pay fines by mail, or directly into the hands of the clerk of the court.

Mail   There are mail drops at each of the visitor centers. Springdale's post office (zip code 84767) is located at 625 Zion Park Blvd., open Monday through Saturday.

At press time, domestic postage rates were 29¢ for a postcard and 44¢ for a letter. For international mail, a first-class letter of up to 1 ounce costs 98¢ (80¢ to Canada and Mexico); a first-class postcard costs the same as a letter. For more information go to **www.usps.com**.

If you aren't sure what your address will be in the United States, mail can be sent to you, in your name, c/o General Delivery at the main post office of the city or region where you expect to be. (Call 📞 **800/275-8777** for information on the nearest post office.) The addressee must pick up mail in person and must produce proof of identity (driver's license, passport, etc.). Most post offices will hold mail for up to 1 month, and are open Monday to Friday from 8am to 5 or 6pm, and Saturday from 8am to noon or a bit later.

Always include zip codes when mailing items in the U.S. If you don't know your zip code, visit www.usps.com/zip4.

Medical Services   The **Zion Canyon Medical Clinic,** 120 Lion Blvd., Springdale (📞 **435/772-3226**), is a family-practice and urgent-care facility. For medical emergencies, dial 📞 **911,** or locate the nearest park ranger. One of the larger hospitals in this part of the state, with a 24-hour emergency room, is **Dixie Regional Medical Center,** 544 S. 400 East, St. George (📞 **435/251-1000;** www.intermountainhealthcare.org). From the east entrance, the nearest medical facility is **Kane County Hospital,** 355 N. Main St., Kanab (📞 **435/644-5811;** www.kchosp.net), which also has a 24-hour emergency room.

For foreign visitors: Unless you're arriving from a nation suffering from an epidemic (particularly cholera or yellow fever), inoculations or vaccinations are not required for entry into the United States.

Mobile Phones   Both GSM and CDMA cell phones work in the gateway communities, but service is spotty in the park, and nonexistent in the more remote areas of the park.

Money & Costs   Frommer's lists exact prices in the local currency. The currency conversions quoted above were correct at press time. However, rates fluctuate, so before departing consult a currency

WHAT THINGS COST IN ZION & BRYCE CANYON NATIONAL PARKS

Double room, moderate, in summer	$140–$160
Double room, inexpensive, in summer	$85–$95
Commercial campground, full RV hookups	$30–$35
Three course dinner for one without wine, moderate	$20–$30
Bottle of beer	$3.50–$5
Cup of coffee	$2–$2.50
1 gallon/1 liter of regular gas	$3.80/$1

exchange website such as **www.oanda.com/currency/converter** to check current rates.

For help with currency conversions, tip calculations, and more, get Frommer's Travel Tools app for your mobile device. Go to www.frommers.com/go/mobile and click on "Travel Tools."

The Value of U.S. Dollars vs. Other Popular Currencies

US$	Aus$	Can$	Euro (€)	NZ$	UK£
$1	A$.94	C$.98	€.71	NZ$1.18	£.62

Packing When packing, keep in mind that this is a land of extremes, with an often-unforgiving climate and terrain. Those planning to hike or bike should take more drinking water containers than they think they'll need—experts recommend at least 1 gallon of water per person per day on the trail—as well as sun block, hats, other protective clothing, and sunglasses with UV protection.

Summer visitors will want to carry rain gear for the typical afternoon thunderstorms, and jackets or sweaters for cool evenings. Winter visitors will not only want warm parkas and hats, but lighter clothing as well—the bright sun at midday can make it feel like June.

Take a first-aid kit, of course, and make sure it contains tweezers—very useful for removing cactus spines. Hikers, especially those planning to go into the Narrows at Zion, will appreciate having a walking stick to brace themselves against the sometimes strong currents on the "trail," which is actually more wading than hiking

Passports Virtually every air traveler entering the U.S. is required to show a passport. All persons, including U.S. citizens, traveling by air between the United States and Canada, Mexico, Central and South America, the Caribbean, and Bermuda are required to present a valid passport. ***Note:*** U.S. and Canadian citizens entering the U. S. at land and sea ports of entry from within the western hemisphere must now also present a passport or other documents compliant with the Western Hemisphere Travel Initiative (WHTI; see www.getyouhome.gov for details). Children 15 and under may continue entering with only a U.S. birth certificate, or other proof of U.S. citizenship.

Passport Offices

- **Australia** Australian Passport Information Service (📞 **131-232,** or visit www.passports.gov.au).
- **Canada Passport Office,** Department of Foreign Affairs and International Trade, Ottawa, ON K1A 0G3 (📞 **800/567-6868;** www.ppt.gc.ca).
- **Ireland Passport Office,** Setanta Centre, Molesworth Street, Dublin 2 (📞 **01/671-1633;** www.foreignaffairs.gov.ie).
- **New Zealand Passports Office,** Department of Internal Affairs, 47 Boulcott Street, Wellington, 6011 (📞 **0800/225-050** in New Zealand or 04/474-8100; www.passports.govt.nz).
- **United Kingdom** Visit your nearest passport office, major post office, or travel agency or contact the **Identity and Passport Service (IPS),** 89 Eccleston Square, London, SW1V 1PN (📞 **0300/222-0000;** www.ips.gov.uk).
- **United States** To find your regional passport office, check the U.S. State Department website (travel.state.gov/passport) or call the **National Passport Information Center** (📞 **877/487-2778**) for automated information.

Petrol Please see "Getting Around by Car," earlier in this chapter.

Police See "Emergencies," earlier in this section.

Safety See "Protecting Your Health & Safety," earlier in this chapter.

Senior Travel See "Passes Offer Free Admission on Most Federal Lands," earlier in the chapter.

Supplies You'll find most of the groceries and camping supplies you want just outside the park's south entrance at **Sol Foods Park Market,** 95 Zion Park Blvd. (📞 **435/772-0277;** www.solfoods.com). This well-stocked store has a good selection of groceries, including fresh produce, meats, and dairy products, plus a very good deli. It also stocks camping supplies, souvenirs, and digital memory cards; rents DVDs; and has a restaurant. It is open daily year-round, 8am to 10pm in summer with shorter hours at other times. In downtown Springdale, you'll find an even better selection at **Sol Foods Downtown Supermarket,** which carries conventional groceries plus organic food and gourmet items, at 995 Zion Park Blvd. (📞 **435/772-3100;** www.solfoods.com). It's open daily 7am to 11pm. On the south end of Springdale (the opposite side of town from the national park), is the **Springdale Fruit Company,** 2491 Zion Park Blvd. (📞 **435/772-3222;** www.springdalefruit.com), which is open only from mid-March through mid-November (daily 9am–7pm) and sells fresh organic fruits, vegetables, and juices (try the fruit smoothies), plus trail mix and baked goods. It also has a picnic area and free Wi-Fi.

Those in need of outdoor equipment, hiking boots, clothing, sleeping bags, stoves, and the like will find what they need at **Zion Outdoor,** 868 Zion Park Blvd. (✆ **435/772-0630;** www.zionoutdoor. com). Outdoor equipment rentals can be found at **Zion Adventure Company,** 36 Lion Blvd. (✆ **435/772-1001;** www.zionadventures. com); and **Zion Rock & Mountain Guides,** 1458 Zion Park Blvd. (✆ **435/772-3303;** www.zionrockguides.com), which rents and sells. For bike rentals and repairs, stop at **Zion Cycles,** also at 868 Zion Park Blvd. (✆ **435/772-0400;** www.zioncycles.com).

Taxes   The United States has no value-added tax (VAT) or other indirect tax at the national level. Every state, county, and city may levy its own local tax on all purchases, including hotel and restaurant checks and airline tickets. These taxes will not appear on price tags.

Telephones   Public telephones are located at the visitor center, Zion Lodge, and the Zion Human History Museum.

Many convenience groceries and packaging services sell **prepaid calling cards** in denominations up to $50. Many public pay phones at airports now accept American Express, MasterCard, and Visa. **Local calls** made from most pay phones cost either 25¢ or 35¢. Most long-distance and international calls can be dialed directly from any phone. **To make calls within the United States and to Canada,** dial 1 followed by the area code and the seven-digit number. **For other international calls,** dial 011 followed by the country code, city code, and the number you are calling.

Calls to area codes **800, 888, 877,** and **866** are toll-free.

For **reversed-charge or collect calls,** and for person-to-person calls, dial the number 0 then the area code and number; an operator will come on the line, and you should specify whether you are calling collect, person-to-person, or both. If your operator-assisted call is international, ask for the overseas operator.

For **directory assistance** ("Information"), dial 411 for local numbers and national numbers in the U.S. and Canada. For dedicated long-distance information, dial 1, then the area code plus 555-1212.

Time   The continental United States is divided into **four time zones:** Eastern Standard Time (EST), Central Standard Time (CST), Mountain Standard Time (MST), and Pacific Standard Time (PST). Alaska and Hawaii have their own zones. For example, when it's 9am in Los Angeles (PST), it's 7am in Honolulu (HST),10am in Denver (MST), 11am in Chicago (CST), noon in New York City (EST), 5pm in London (GMT), and 2am the next day in Sydney.

All of Utah is in the Mountain Standard Time zone.

Daylight saving time (summer time) is in effect from 1am on the second Sunday in March to 1am on the first Sunday in November, except in Arizona, Hawaii, the U.S. Virgin Islands, and Puerto Rico. Daylight saving time moves the clock 1 hour ahead of standard time.

For help with time translations, download our Travel Tools app for your mobile device. Go to www.frommers.com/go/mobile and click on the Travel Tools icon.

Tipping   In hotels, tip **bellhops** at least $1 per bag ($2–$3 if you have a lot of luggage) and tip the **chamber staff** $1 to $2 per day (more if you've left a big mess for him or her to clean up). Tip the **doorman** or **concierge** only if he or she has provided you with some specific service (for example, calling a cab for you or obtaining difficult-to-get theater tickets). Tip the **valet-parking attendant** $1 every time you get your car.

In restaurants, bars, and nightclubs, tip **service staff** and **bartenders** 15% to 20% of the check, tip **checkroom attendants** $1 per garment, and tip **valet-parking attendants** $1 per vehicle.

As for other service personnel, tip **cab drivers** 15% of the fare; tip **skycaps** at airports at least $1 per bag ($2–$3 if you have a lot of luggage); and tip **hairdressers** and **barbers** 15% to 20%.

For help with tip calculations, currency conversions, and more, download the Travel Tools app for your mobile device (see above).

Toilets   See "Where to Find Restrooms in Zion," (p. 20).

VAT   See "Taxes," earlier in this section.

Visas   The U.S. State Department has a **Visa Waiver Program (VWP)** allowing citizens of the following countries to enter the United States without a visa for stays of up to 90 days: Andorra, Australia, Austria, Belgium, Brunei, Czech Republic, Denmark, Estonia, Finland, France, Germany, Greece, Hungary, Iceland, Ireland, Italy, Japan, Latvia, Liechtenstein, Lithuania, Luxembourg, Malta, Monaco, the Netherlands, New Zealand, Norway, Portugal, San Marino, Singapore, Slovakia, Slovenia, South Korea, Spain, Sweden, Switzerland, and the United Kingdom. (**Note:** This list was accurate at press time; for the most up-to-date list of countries in the VWP, consult http://travel.state.gov/visa.) Even though a visa isn't necessary, in an effort to help U.S. officials check travelers against terror watch lists before they arrive at U.S. borders, visitors from VWP countries must register online through the Electronic System for Travel Authorization (ESTA) before boarding a plane or a boat to the U.S. Travelers must complete an electronic application providing basic personal and travel eligibility information. The Department of Homeland Security recommends filling out the form at least three days before traveling. Authorizations will be valid for up to two years or until the traveler's passport expires, whichever comes first. Currently, there is 1 US$14 fee for the online application. Existing ESTA registrations remain valid through their expiration dates. **Note:** Any passport issued on or after October 26, 2006, by a VWP country must be an **e-Passport** for VWP travelers to be eligible to enter the U.S. without a visa. Citizens of these nations also need to present a round-trip air or cruise ticket upon arrival. E-Passports contain computer chips capable of storing biometric information, such as the required digital photograph of the holder. If your passport doesn't have this feature, you can still travel without a visa if the valid passport was issued before October 26, 2005, and includes a machine-readable zone; or if the valid passport was issued between October 26, 2005, and October 25, 2006, and includes a digital photograph. For more information, go to **http://travel.state. gov/visa**. Canadian citizens may enter the United States without visas, but will need to show passports and proof of residence.

Citizens of all other countries must have (1) a valid passport that expires at least 6 months later than the scheduled end of their visit to the U.S.; and (2) a tourist visa.

For information about U.S. Visas go to **http://travel.state.gov** and click on "Visas." Or go to one of the following websites:

Australian citizens can obtain up-to-date visa information from the **U.S. Embassy Canberra,** Moonah Place, Yarralumla, ACT 2600 (📞 **02/6214-5600**) or by checking the U.S. Diplomatic Mission's website at **http://canberra.usembassy.gov/visas.html**.

British subjects can obtain up-to-date visa information by calling the **U.S. Embassy Visa Information Line** (📞 **09042-450-100** from within the U.K. at £1.20 per minute; or 📞 **866-382-3589** from within the U.S. at a flat rate of $16 and is payable by credit card only) or by visiting the "Visas to the U.S." section of the American Embassy London's website at **http://london.usembassy.gov/visas.html**.

Irish citizens can obtain up-to-date visa information through the **U.S. Embassy Dublin,** 42 Elgin Rd., Ballsbridge, Dublin 4 (📞 1580-47-VISA [8472] from within the Republic of Ireland at €2.40 per minute; **http://dublin.usembassy.gov**).

Citizens of **New Zealand** can obtain up-to-date visa information by contacting the **U.S. Embassy New Zealand,** 29 Fitzherbert Terrace, Thorndon, Wellington (📞 **644/462-6000; http://newzealand. usembassy.gov**).

Visitor Information   Contact Zion National Park, Springdale, UT 84767 (📞 **435/772-3256;** www.nps.gov/zion). Officials will mail you information (they request that you write rather than call, at least a month before your planned visit), but you will find everything they will send you and more at the park website. You can also get information at www.twitter.com/zionnps and see a variety of photos at www. flickr.com/photos/zionnps.

You can purchase books, posters, maps, DVDs, and CDs related to the park from the nonprofit **Zion Natural History Association,** Zion National Park, Springdale, UT 84767 (📞 **800/635-3959** or 435/772-3265; www.zionpark.org). Some publications are available in foreign languages, including German, French, Japanese, and Chinese. Those wanting to help the nonprofit association can join ($45 single or $60 family annually) and get a 20% discount on purchases, a 20% discount on most Zion Canyon Field Institute classes, and discounts at most other nonprofit bookstores at national parks, monuments, historic sites, and recreation areas.

Among the publications available from the Zion Natural History Association is the inexpensive and easy-to-understand 22-page booklet *An Introduction to the Geology of Zion National Park,* by Al Warneke. Those who want more information, plus some spectacular photos, should consider *Water, Rock & Time: The Geologic Story of Zion National Park,* by Dr. Robert L. Eves. With a foreword by Robert Redford, *A Century of Sanctuary—The Art of Zion National Park* is a beautiful collection of about 140 historic and contemporary paintings depicting the park plus five essays. There are also a number of detailed hiking guides and specialized books on the area's plants and animals.

Those planning to spend a lot of time in the backcountry on Zion's trails should purchase the *Trails Illustrated* topographic map.

For additional information about the area contact the **Zion Canyon Visitors Bureau,** P.O. Box 331, Springdale, UT 84767 (© **888/518-7070;** www.zionpark.com).

Weather   For current statewide weather information, contact the **National Weather Service** (© **801/524-5133;** www.wrh.noaa.gov/slc). For local weather information, call the park office at © **435/772-3256.**

Wi-Fi   See "Internet & Wi-Fi," earlier in this section.

[FastFACTS] BRYCE CANYON NATIONAL PARK

Area Codes   The area code is 435.

ATMs   Just outside the entrance to the park, there is an automated teller machine (ATM) in the lobby of **Ruby's Inn** (© **866/866-6616** or 435/834-5341; www.rubysinn.com).

Car Rental   See "Getting There by Car," earlier in this chapter.

Cellphones   See "Mobile Phones," later in this section.

Disabled Travelers   The National Park Service has made great strides in recent years in making their facilities more accessible to those with disabilities. The Bryce Canyon Visitor Center is wheelchair accessible, including the restrooms. A half-mile section of the Rim Trail, between Sunrise and Sunset Points, is fairly level, paved, and wheelchair accessible; several of the viewpoints along the scenic drive are accessible; the Bristlecone Loop Trail, at Rainbow Point, has a hard surface and is accessible with assistance; Sunset Campground has accessible campsites, and the shuttle bus is completely accessible. Also, park rangers are extremely receptive to helping disabled travelers. Those with disabilities can obtain free admission and discounts on many park facilities, such as campgrounds. See "Passes Offer Free Admission on Most Federal Lands," earlier in the chapter.

The Utah information and referral line for people with disabilities is 📞 **800/333-8824**, or go online to www.accessut.org.

Doctors   See "Medical Services," later in this section.

Drinking Laws   Please see this subject in "Fast Facts: Zion National Park," above.

Driving Rules   See "Getting Around," earlier in this chapter.

Electricity   Please see this subject in "Fast Facts: Zion National Park," above.

Embassies & Consulates   Please see this subject in "Fast Facts: Zion National Park," above.

Emergencies   Dial 📞 **911,** 435/676-2411, or contact a park ranger.

Family Travel   Visiting Bryce Canyon National Park with your children can be an especially rewarding experience, and is an excellent way for everyone to learn about the park's geology, plants, and animals, as well as to appreciate the unequaled beauty of nature.

However, the park is in a rural area, and nearby communities offer the basics but little else. There are no major chain grocers or discount stores, and although you will be able to buy items such as baby food and disposable diapers, you may not find the variety that you're used to. Parents should have a good supply of these items with them, stocking up in larger communities such as Las Vegas, Salt Lake City, or St. George. Carry any prescription drugs you might need, and make sure you have phone numbers for your doctor and pharmacist.

To locate accommodations, restaurants, and attractions that are kid-friendly, look for the "Kids" icon throughout this guide.

Gasoline   Please see "Getting Around by Car," earlier in this chapter.

Health   Please see "Protecting Your Health & Safety," earlier in this chapter.

Hospitals   See "Medical Services," later in this section.

Insurance   For information on traveler's insurance, trip cancellation insurance, and medical insurance while traveling, please visit www.frommers.com/planning.

Internet & Wi-Fi   Free Wi-Fi access is available year-round at the visitor center and from April through October in the Lodge at Bryce Canyon lobby and the front porch of the General Store. Most lodging facilities discussed in chapter 7 also offer free Wi-Fi.

Laundry   Inside the park, there is a coin-operated laundry at the General Store, about a quarter-mile south of North Campground, near the Sunrise Point parking area. It's open daily from mid-April to October.

Just outside the entrance to the park, Ruby's Inn has two coin-operated laundry facilities. The one in the main complex is open 24 hours a day year-round, and the second, located at Ruby's

Campground, about a quarter-mile south of the inn, is open April through October from 7am to 9:30pm daily.

Legal Aid   Please see this subject in "Fast Facts: Zion National Park," above.

Mail   A U.S. Post Office is located inside the main building of Ruby's Inn, just outside the park in Bryce Canyon City (zip code 84764). Also, please see this subject in "Fast Facts: Zion National Park," above.

Medical Services   A first-aid station is at the Lodge at Bryce Canyon. The closest hospital is **Garfield Memorial Hospital,** 200 N. 400 E., in Panguitch, 24 miles northwest via Utah 12 and U.S. 89 (*©* **435/676-8811;** www.intermountainhealthcare.org), which has a 24-hour emergency room.

For foreign visitors: Unless you're arriving from an area suffering from an epidemic (particularly cholera or yellow fever), inoculations or vaccinations are not required for entry into the United States.

Mobile Phones   Both GSM and CDMA cell phones work in the gateway communities, but service is spotty in the park, and nonexistent in the more remote areas of the park.

Money & Costs   See "Fast Facts: Zion National Park," above.

Packing   See "Fast Facts: Zion National Park," above.

Passports   See "Fast Facts: Zion National Park," above.

Petrol   See "Getting Around by Car," earlier in this chapter.

Police   See "Emergencies," earlier in this section.

Safety   See "Protecting Your Health & Safety," earlier in this chapter.

Senior Travel   See "Passes Offer Free Admission on Most Federal Lands," earlier in the chapter.

Supplies   There is a small General Store (contact the **Lodge at Bryce Canyon,** *©* **435/834-8700;** www.brycecanyonforever.com) inside the park that is open daily from mid-May to mid-October (call for hours), with groceries and camping supplies, plus snacks, ice, beer, bundles of firewood, and souvenirs, all at surprisingly reasonable prices. The General Store is about a quarter-mile south of North Campground near the Sunrise Point parking area.

On the south side of the lobby of **Ruby's Inn** (*©* **866/866-6616** or 435/834-5484; www.rubysinn.com), just outside the entrance to the park, is a huge general store that offers souvenirs, Western clothing, camping supplies, and a good selection of groceries. The store is open from 7am to 10:30pm daily. In the lobby are a small liquor store, a car-rental desk, a beauty salon, a photo shop with digital photo services, and tour desks where you can arrange excursions, from horseback treks and all-terrain-vehicle rides to helicopter tours.

Taxes   See "Fast Facts: Zion National Park," above.

Telephones Public telephones are at the visitor center, the Lodge at Bryce Canyon, and the General Store. There is also a public phone at Ruby's Inn, just north of the park entrance. See "Fast Facts: Zion National Park," above.

Time See "Fast Facts: Zion National Park," above.

Tipping See "Fast Facts: Zion National Park," above.

Toilets See "Restrooms at Bryce Canyon" (p. 20).

VAT See "Taxes," earlier in this section.

Visas See "Fast Facts: Zion National Park," above.

Visitor Information For advance information on what to see and do in **Bryce Canyon National Park,** contact the park at P.O. Box 640201, Bryce, UT 84764-0201 (© **435/834-5322;** www.nps.gov/brca). Officials request that you write rather than call, at least a month before your planned visit, for them to mail information. However, you will find everything they will send you and more at the park website. You can also get information at www.twitter.com/brycecanyonnps and at www.facebook.com/brycecanyonnps.

For even more details, order books, maps, posters, DVDs, videotapes, and CDs from the nonprofit **Bryce Canyon Natural History Association,** P.O. Box 640051, Bryce, UT 84764-0051 (© **888/362-2642** or 435/834-4782; www.brycecanyon.org). Association members ($35 single or $50 family annually) receive a 15% discount on purchases and discounts for programs presented by the High Plateaus Institute. Members also receive discounts at the Bryce Lodge gift shop and most other nonprofit bookstores at national parks, monuments, historic sites, and recreation areas.

Among the books that the association sells is the excellent *Hiking Zion & Bryce Canyon National Parks,* by Erik Molvar and Tamara Martin, which includes detailed trail descriptions for both parks. *The Bryce Canyon Auto and Hiking Guide,* by Tully Stroud and Paul R. Johnson, is published by the association and has discussions of the various viewpoints and hiking trails, a variety of color photos of the park, and historic black-and-white photos. The association publishes *Shadows of Time: The Geology of Bryce Canyon National Park,* by Frank DeCourten, John Telford, and Hannah Hinchman.

For additional information on the area, contact **Bryce Canyon Country,** operated by the Garfield County Office of Tourism (© **800/444-6689** or 435/676-1102; www.brycecanyoncountry.com).

Weather For current statewide weather information, contact the **National Weather Service** (© **801/524-5133;** www.wrh.noaa.gov/slc). For local weather information, call the park office (© **435/834-5322**).

Wi-Fi See "Internet & Wi-Fi," earlier in this section.

Index

See also Accommodations and Restaurant indexes, below.

General Index